WHAT PEOPLE A

MINDFULNESS

With a rare combination of intellectual clarity and heartfelt practicality, Ira Rechtshaffer applies Buddhist wisdom to the down-to-earth issues of daily life. His deep feeling for the sacred illuminates the powerful path he lays out for personal healing, transformation, and freedom. A gem of a book... really something special here!

Rick Hanson, Ph.D., author of *Buddha's Brain: The Practical Neuroscience of Happiness, Love, and Wisdom*

A wise and mature book, filled with fresh metaphors and insights that breathe new life into age-old Buddhist practices. Nourishing food for thought for those deep in the Buddhist tradition, yet written in a warm and personal tone that will appeal to all who are curious about Buddhism. Inquiring minds, apply within!

Tim Ward, author of *What the Buddha Never Taught* and *Indestructible You: Building a Self that Can't be Broken*

Mindfulness and Madness is at once both a comprehensive introduction to the power of mindfulness and an in-depth exploration of Buddhist thought and practice. Teaching stories bring Buddhist principles to life, and Rechtshaffer's years of experience as a meditation teacher and psychotherapist shine through his highly intelligent prose. A fabulous addition to any seeker's library!

Ann Betz, PCC, CPCC

Based on years of experience as a psychotherapist and a life-long meditation practice, Ira Rechtshaffer has shown how both traditions combine to contribute to easing human suffering. He leads a reader along a path of discovery of the elements which make up a personal identity, its struggles and the possibility of surcease. The book concludes with a delightful way of looking at personality in terms of the six Buddhist realms. From narcissism to neurosis, Rechtshaffer shows how mindfulness can heal our estrangement from ourselves.

Dr. Charles Fisher, Prof. Emeritus Brandeis University

Mindfulness and Madness is a beautiful book describing the power of mindfulness and its healing properties. And yet, at the same time, it's a book about us: the madness in the way we lead our lives, the crazy fast-pace that creates disconnection with ourselves and our environment. If you wish to transform your life from the mad into the mindful this book would be a wonderful gift to yourself.

Dr Itai Ivtzan, Senior Lecturer Positive Psychology
Programme Leader: MAPP.

Mindfulness and Madness

Money, Food, Sex and the Sacred

Mindfulness and Madness

Money, Food, Sex and the Sacred

Ira Rechtshaffer Ph.D.

CHANGE
MAKERS
BOOKS

Winchester, UK
Washington, USA

First published by Changemakers Books, 2015
Changemakers Books is an imprint of John Hunt Publishing Ltd., Laurel House, Station Approach,
Alresford, Hants, SO24 9JH, UK
office1@jhpbooks.net
www.johnhuntpublishing.com
www.changemakers-books.com

For distributor details and how to order please visit the 'Ordering' section on our website.

Text copyright: Ira Rechtshaffer 2014

ISBN: 978 1 78535 086 3
Library of Congress Control Number: 2015937449

A CIP catalogue record for this book is available from the British Library.

Design: Stuart Davies

Printed and bound by CPI Group (UK) Ltd, Croydon, CR0 4YY, UK

We operate a distinctive and ethical publishing philosophy in all
areas of our business, from our global network of authors to
production and worldwide distribution.

CONTENTS

This book is dedicated to the incomparable spiritual warrior, Chogyam Trungpa Rinpoche, who showed me the way, and to the many teachers from the various schools of Buddhism who have carried the Buddha's teachings of liberation to the West for the benefit of all.

Acknowledgments

I would like to offer great thanks and appreciation to Sarah Holman for her tireless efforts in transcribing my dharma talks which became the basis for this present book. I would also like to express my appreciation for the group of men and women who have come together to form a sangha, a community of mindfulness practitioners, to whom these dharma talks were given. Their openness, inquisitiveness and commitment were the magnet that inspired these talks.

If you are interested in training programs based on the principles and practices in this book, please visit my website: irarecht-shaffer.com or email me at irarex108@att.net

Introduction

We've been fortunate to have had many great Buddhist teachers who began coming to the West since the 1960s, and many Westerners like myself who had the auspicious occasion to become students of such teachers and receive their profound instructions. We learned how to relate with this tradition as a way of life and not merely as a set of techniques for self-improvement. The good news is that the teachings of the Buddha, the Buddha dharma, are continuing to be transplanted in the soil of our Western culture, and the recipe for how to walk this brilliant path remains up to date and accessible. One need not be a Buddhist to take advantage of this feast of precious teachings. The central or core practice within all the Buddhist lineages is mindfulness meditation.

Mindfulness is our human capacity to give full attention to what we're doing at the moment, without allowing random thoughts to distract us. It is complete involvement in any activity. As an intentional practice, mindfulness is universal and is part of all genuine endeavors, secular and spiritual.

On the Buddhist path, mindfulness training is aimed at freeing us from unnecessary suffering by bringing both our mind and body into the present moment. This intentional practice begins with seated meditation. As practitioners, we sit in silence and stillness while placing our attention on the rhythmic cycles of breathing, as a reminder to stay present. Within this simple activity we pay attention to what we rarely give a moment's thought to: *nowness*, what is arising in *this* moment. This could be the arising of a thought, a feeling or a bodily sensation in our belly.

The key to Buddhist mindfulness practice is to remember to let go of what we just noticed and to place our whole attention on what is arising in *each* succeeding moment. We don't judge or analyze our thoughts, but simply observe them and let go. The gift of mindfulness meditation is that it offers a fresh glimpse of both ourselves and our world. Buddhists call this naked perception.

Mindfulness meditation involves the paradox of both having control over our mind and simultaneously abandoning ourselves to its ongoing display. This is a practice of walking the razor's edge between not too tight and not too loose. By continuously remembering to be present we experience a refreshing sense of being awake, alive and peaceful.

This quality of direct contact with the truth of our immediate situation stands in contrast with 'madness', which is to be 'out of our mind', elsewhere, distracted and confused. Madness is when we are having breakfast while watching CNN on our laptop, and planning the rest of our day in our mind. We barely taste the fresh fruit in our bowl or feel its texture or delight in its fragrance or visual appeal. Madness is the state of mind that is obsessed, preoccupied or emotionally reactive and therefore 'blinded' to the truth of the situation at hand. We tend to project this scattered state of mind onto the empty canvas of ordinary situations and create confusion for ourselves and others.

The problem is that we are blind in regard to our own blindness. Most of us don't realize how much of our lives are spent mindlessly, identified with our own internal gossip or cognitive muzak. Over time this leaves us with a feeling that something is missing from our experience. Our effort to compensate for what seems to be a lack or an absence provokes us to look for gratification in all the wrong places.

Madness or neurotic behavior creates suffering, but also provokes the deep desire to be free of suffering. One of the underlying themes of this book is that if we neither deny our dissatisfaction nor fight with it, but witness ourselves with penetrating mindfulness, we can begin to understand how we contribute to our own anguish. The paradox is that madness may lead to liberation from madness.

The usual sense of 'mind' is the familiar experience of silently talking to ourselves, having multiple conversations going on all throughout the day. Mindfulness permits us to objectively witness our self-talk without becoming involved with it. As this practice matures we are more able to transcend the 'monkey mind' of forgetfulness, distractibility and reactivity, all of which make our mind neurotic and confused. To be fully present and open, free of whirling thoughts and inner conversations, is to experience oneself as a clearing in the thicket of tangential thoughts.

While mindfulness meditation focuses on the mind's content, a particular thought, image or memory, *awareness* is the larger space of mind within which thoughts and images arise. Awareness provides the meditator with a context and a perspective for the individual thoughts. This larger space becomes the basis for insight.

For example, in one moment we may have a desire for Rocky Road ice cream, while in the next moment, an impulse to leave our job, and in the next moment, a wish to live on a tropical island. Mindfulness perceives the precise images or thoughts without necessarily understanding their implication or suggestion. It is just bare observation. By contrast, awareness recognizes that we are feeling empty and dissatisfied and are fantasizing about change. This offers some insight into our life circumstance or situation. Mindfulness and awareness are complementary aspects of meditation, and like two wings of a bird, allow meditation to take off, so to speak. Throughout the chapters of this book I will emphasize one aspect, while in other instances, the other will be accentuated.

Buddhism in essence is a practical path of liberation from neurosis and its symptoms of anxiety, depression, inertia and dysfunctionality. It is a profound psycho spiritual tool that instructs us how to transmute the raw material of our neurosis into sanity and well-being.

Neurosis, as I am using the term, is a disconnection from our essence or Buddha nature, which creates an inner abyss of painful emptiness. Dissociating from what is most fundamental within us provokes a misguided search to regain what we never really lost. This neurotic search leads to a distortion of our whole personality.

In the Tibetan Buddhist tradition the whole body of the Buddhist teachings or dharma is divided into three yanas or vehicles. These 3 cycles of teachings are referred to as *Hinayana*, *Mahayana* and *Vajrayana*. Using the metaphor of a growing tree, the roots of the Buddhist tree begin with the *Hinayana*, the foundational vehicle, while the powerful trunk would be the *Mahayana*, the larger or expansive vehicle, and the flowering branches would be the *Vajrayana*, the fruitional development and integration of the whole path.

The Hinayana is a *stage* in a developmental process and not to be equated with the Theravadin tradition of Southeast Asia. It is about working with the ingredients of everyday life. It is getting to the truth of our existence as lived right now. How we pour a cup of tea, how we handle money, food or substance, how we deal with loneliness, boredom or anger are all aspects of the Hinayana stage. Mindfulness directs our attention to notice how we are dealing with our moment to moment existence but without judgment or analysis. The Hinayana, the first stage of the Buddhist developmental path, works with our life as it is, and recognizes the futility of trying to be elsewhere.

Beyond working with the roots of our everyday lives, the *Mahayana* or big vehicle, takes a more expansive view of the Buddha's teachings. As mindfulness and awareness mature, we discover a place within ourselves that we can't defend against. This soft spot feels like an open wound and is the source of compassion. Another's pain makes a direct claim upon us and moves us to make a gesture of care. This development is made

4

possible as meditation helps us to shed layer after layer of defense, relaxing our body armor so that the world can get through to touch us.

Mindfulness-awareness practice permits us to glimpse the world beyond our personal story of it. We begin to see beyond our projections, unveiling a naked world, empty of our preoccupations, expectations, and personal narratives. The Mahayana aspect of the path brings the Hinayana teachings to fruition.

At this developmental level we actually cut through the 'us versus them' mentality and gradually open our boundaries so that we include the 'other'. We are challenged to open to friend *and* adversary, this group *and* that group. Mindfulness practice at this level cuts through our tendency to solidify our experience into opposing categories, so that our ego boundaries eventually include more and more of the world.

Remarkably, the Buddhist developmental path suggests further spiritual evolution beyond the Mahayana stage. A *bodhisattva* is a spiritual warrior with an open heart on the Mahayana path who works for the benefit of all beings. But this fervor to be of immense service to the world could go astray and become eccentric. We could 'stink' from too much goodness, too much self-sacrifice, too much spirituality. At this mature level we could still be trying very, very hard. We could find ourselves struggling to roll a huge boulder up an immense hill. There could be a tight fist of effort due to our heavy spiritual agenda. What was once medicine has become poison.

The last yana or vehicle is called the Vajrayana. The Vajrayana is called the path of skillful means. It brings the suggestions of the Mahayana stage to complete fruition. It offers an immense variety of methods to corner and subjugate our spiritualized ego, transforming its energy in the service of a *sacred* view of life. Within the Buddhist tradition we might think of sacredness as a return to innocence. It is pure perception untainted by our personal history and any effort to manipulate There have been moments when we all have intuitively sensed a primordial or timeless quality that radiates an immense depth through the complications of our world. Although inconceivable, such an experience is nevertheless palpable. This is the sacred.

Whether we're balancing our checkbook, dealing with our irate teenage son or daughter, dealing with money problems, traffic problems or relational issues, the sacred dimension frames all of our experiences. We're not trying to escape 'here' to get 'there', because we have finally landed 'here'. We experience ourselves as an embodied presence from which nothing is lacking. This quality of presence elicits the invisible aspect of the world.

The three-yana approach meticulously guides us how to evolve the practice of mindfulness in stages so that we can transform the challenges of everyday life into an expression of freedom and creativity. It teaches us how to open our hearts and bellies, how to relax the tight fist of effort that we all experience, and how to glimpse the sacredness of everyday life. At last, we can be authentically present without apology or explanation. Here there's inspiration to celebrate.

My intention in writing this book is to present the Buddha's dharma using psychological language in a way that is familiar to a modern Western audience, so that the teachings do not feel like an exotic foreign import. Further, I have presented the teachings from a developmental perspective so that the reader can relate with the dharma as a personal journey, starting from where he or she is.

Buddhism's developmental perspective suggests that we can make use of some part of each of the yanas as they speak to us. My hope is that my readers will be able to make use of these teachings as immediately relevant and practical, as they journey in their everyday lives from here to here.

I. The Path of Renunciation

Chapter 1

Mindfulness as the Wisdom of No Escape

The practice of 'being' is a very rare activity. Very few human beings in our postmodern world understand or appreciate the value of sitting attentively in silence and stillness. Mindfulness meditation is like sitting by the bank of a great stream. The stream's strong currents carry our many memories, our rich tapestry of experiences, both painful and pleasurable, as well as our anticipation of what is yet to come.

Our job as meditators is to remain on the bank of the stream and simply observe, without becoming overly fascinated with the psychic jetsam and flotsam. If our attention gets hooked by a provocative thought or image, we immediately fall into this mind stream and become part of the swirling jetsam and flotsam.

The essence of mindfulness practice is *recognizing* that you have fallen into the stream. That very noticing immediately brings you back to your position on the bank as an observer. Don't be discouraged if you find that you spend more time in the stream than on its peaceful shore. Your attention will alternate between witnessing and falling into the stream. That's what Buddhists call the path. If you slip off the horse, you get back on.

It's important to understand that there are not two steps, one of falling into the mind stream, and the other of getting back to the shore. When you see that you've fallen into the stream, that is, that you've become distracted or preoccupied, you're already back on the bank of the stream as an observer. You've come back into presence.

One of the powers of mindfulness practice is that it brings our mind and body together in the same place so that they're synchronized. Basic trust grows from 'staying' and 'not going' because our mind finally catches up with our body. There is a kind of magic in declaring a spot on earth and fully sitting there.

Most of the time our body is in one place and our mind is somewhere else. Our body is sitting and having a cup of coffee, while our mind is preoccupied with our day's agenda or with our unresolved problems and concerns. Few of us realize the implications of this phenomenon. We actually lose trust in ourselves day by day when our body is in one place and our mind is somewhere else.

In the usual state of *mindlessness*, we fully identify with our own rambling, free associative thoughts. They continually trigger a chain reaction of further thoughts, images and feelings and these make up our personal narratives. This is how we manufacture psychological realms of all sorts, which we then *inhabit*. It is these psychological realms that create *samsara* or collective neurosis. In some sense, everyone is living in their own world.

One aspect of mindfulness meditation is the practice of extending unconditional friendliness or loving kindness towards ourselves. This is what restores a sense of basic trust in ourselves again. By sitting in silence and stillness we intentionally invite openness in the midst of the frenetic speed of everyday life.

In practicing *mindfulness of body* we establish a foundation, a home ground. With that comes a sense of being settled. We start by assuming a good upright posture, either on a meditation cushion or in a supportive chair. We anchor our attention in our body, so that little by little, we come down from the cloud realm of discursive thinking and land in our body.

We feel our body and the movement of breath. There is an unmistakable sense of simple presence. "I am here, now". Our breath moves in and out like the rhythmic tides of the ocean. Our heart beats and circulates blood, while the miracles of sight, sound, smell, taste and feeling all take place effortlessly. No matter what thought, image or memory arises in the space of mind, we do not identify with it. We simply sit, breathe and are present.

Instead, we align ourselves with the awareness that witnesses such mental phenomena. We identify with the mirroring aspect of mind, and not the images that appear to the mirror. In this way we begin to establish some sense of presence in spite of all the stuff going on in our mind.

The cyclical movement of breath itself is the epitome of the life force that animates all living entities. 'Letting go' means that we can trust this natural rhythmic process without attempting to secure it. Like the rhythmic rising and falling of the oceanic tides, the circulation of inhalation and exhalation is trustworthy and beyond our need to control it. We place our attention on this natural movement and this permits us to stay more focused. We are present with posture and breath, and when something arises in our state of mind, we notice and then we let go. 'Letting go' must be applied uniformly even to the meditative state itself. We do not try to *capture* such positive moments, but touch this peaceful state of mind with awareness and then let go.

Mindfulness is a sudden flash of recognition, a complete reversal of direction bringing us instantly back to the breath. By interrupting our storylines, our compelling narratives of love and desire, hope and fear, success and the anguish of failure, we are brought back to the immediacy of this present moment. Only one thing is happening at a time. The practice of mindfulness is to be there with that precise, abrupt perception of *nowness* from which there is no escape. That dimensionless point of awareness is the key to our true identity.

As our mindfulness meditation evolves we experience a kind of radiation that is felt as an energetic presence. That energetic presence feels fundamentally healthy, intelligent and friendly. It is a sense of open heartedness and basic dignity. When this basic energetic presence meets with our wounds, healing happens. Meditation is a radically open and tender state of mind. Whatever needs our attention can arise in a space of acceptance and loving kindness, so that even our wounds may express themselves without retraumatizing us. We touch them with awareness and let them go. The open hearted tenderness of mindfulness is the one thing that actually does heal.

Chapter 2

Tender Courage

Mindfulness meditation suggests that it is refreshing to meet the nakedness of situations with your own nakedness, here and now. Outside of the immediacy of nowness we fail to genuinely appreciate our lives because we are struggling to survive in time, projecting ourselves into the future or attempting to resolve the past.

There are so many ideas for how to be a human being, so many perspectives on what a human being actually is. There are socio-economic, anthropological, psychological, and biological perspectives, as well as gender, religious, racial and nationalistic frames of reference, just to name a few. You could even have Ph.Ds in multiple disciplines and still not truly understand why you're here on this earth and what your real purpose is.

As spiritual practitioners it is necessary to question who we are in essence, beyond our social roles as parents, spouses, family members, friends and colleagues, and beyond our occupational roles. What *is* this human life really about?

The good news is that the tradition of Buddhism addresses this question by offering a method of inquiry. Mindfulness meditation is a profound practice that has come down to us from 2600 years ago. We have the recipe for how to *discover* our essential nature as a human being. We do not have to conduct an archaeological dig for ancient relics, to crack the mystery of our true identity. If you give yourself to the practice of mindfulness wholeheartedly, you will meet yourself face to face.

In this moment if you allow yourself to become sensitive to your immediate condition, you will discover that you are breathing with ease. You might notice also that your chest and abdomen are rising and falling rhythmically with the cyclical movement of breath. You are not required to perform the activity of breathing, for it is already handled by your autonomic nervous system, as is the beating of your heart and the circulation of your blood. You are not required to struggle to maintain your existence.

At this moment you might notice a panoramic view of rolling hills or a skyline of skyscrapers out your window and hear the hum of cars on the freeway. It is not necessary to struggle to see the landscape or hear the cars any better than you already do.

I have been describing *basic being*, the most fundamental sense of what it is to be a human being. This quality of *being* exists before we divided the world into good and bad, inner and outer, past and future. No one owns this basic being and yet it is the very essence of who we are.

Basic being is the human capacity to experience 'things as they are' before we project our labels onto them. We could call this naked experience *isness* or *suchness*, which is a translation of the Sanskrit term, *tathata*. The secret for how to experience this natural quality is to completely open to this arising moment, right now, this second! If you look through the frame of the next moment, hoping to contact the previous moment, then you are looking in your rearview mirror watching the scenery that has just passed. You now have a reflection, a memory, or an idea of basic being, not the actual experience of basic *isness* itself.

This quality of basic being can only be experienced now (snaps fingers) in this living moment. It arises and dissolves like the flashing of light in the sky. Moment by moment, we have an opportunity to open to that basic sense of being, but we must leave our agendas behind, and we must let go of our personal narrative with its long compelling case history.

In the moment that we touch it, we must also refrain from holding onto it, from trying to make it our personal territory. We touch the immediacy of this living moment and let go, trusting that it will return. Usually we slip off that razor-sharp edge of nowness due to our habitual hunger for distraction and entertainment. We're not sure how to name this loss of balance, or whether to even call it a problem since this seems so normal. But this so-called normalcy is sheer madness. It is the unconscious rejection of the 'here and now' in favor of the 'then and there'.

When we're not living in the immediacy of now, there's a feeling that we're distant from the hot center of our lives. We feel disconnected from the joy that we may have remembered as kids, that free-floating spontaneous sense of 'mindless' happiness. To miss these precious moments means that we are lost in action, hitchhiking between memory and desire.

The practice of mindfulness meditation returns us again and again to this basic space of nowness from which our lives unfold. This basic space is none other than Buddha nature and it is our natural inheritance as human beings. Sometimes this natural inheritance feels like hidden treasure, buried deep and outside of our ordinary lives. When we are not connected to it we may find ourselves rolling an enormous boulder up the hill of our lives in order to *earn* the right to be here.

Most people feel driven from within, struggling with inner demands to either be more or have more, or to resolve past problems or anticipate future ones. Alternatively, many struggle with that boulder in order to exhaust themselves into numbness and insensitivity in order to minimize the pain of emptiness, aimlessness and meaninglessness.

Buddhism states that although wisdom, compassion and peacefulness are our fundamental inheritance as human beings, we mistakenly identify Buddha nature with the ego-self, our mental picture of ourselves, which is only a fragment of our inconceivable totality. We throw ourselves into our various social roles and functions and their various scripts, as husband or father, a wife or mother, engineer or office worker, and lose that fluid sense of open possibility.

Regular mindfulness practice gradually reveals that as we open to our depths we may feel mysteriously gratified for simply being here, now. We may not know how to put words to our experience of simplicity, openness, and clear perception. The Buddhist tradition teaches that our authentic nature can only be discovered in *nowness,* which exists moment by moment, before the next thought, before you utter a word, or reach for the next cup of coffee.

This sense of basic being is not a thing, but an essential capacity to experience life without filters. The dimension within us that is *being* has depth, value, relatedness, and real substance. It is a sense of presentness and presence. The secret is that it is revealed only when we show up in our totality, with our head, heart, and belly.

The conventional world in which we live is terrified of vulnerability because it views ordinary life as a Darwinian jungle where only the clever and the strong survive and where struggle and aggression are appropriate. If we identify as a struggling animal trying to survive in a social jungle, we lose that sense of softness, tenderness and sympathy towards ourselves and others. We begin to take existence for granted and miss the opportunity to appreciate ourselves and the natural world in which we live.

Because so many of us are challenged by our own fear of survival, we need to cultivate an attitude of courage. This means not being afraid of who we are. When we feel afraid of ourselves we also feel threatened by the world. We then want to build little havens of comfort so we can hide both from ourselves and the world.

Courage is necessary to investigate and see objectively what's really going on with ourselves. It takes tender courage to sit and face our fears and our depressions, to discover the deepest elements of mind and body without trying to change them, in order to see the truth of 'what is'. Such tender courage allows us to cultivate deep listening from the heart from where we might discover that we have spent a lifetime completely identified with the internal 'chatter box' in our head. This discovery provokes us to question: "Is that all there is to me, endless loops of discursive thoughts?" "Am I really defined by these habitual patterns of thought and feeling?"

The discovery of awakened heart comes from first allowing space so that we can appreciate very simple experiences. The most fundamental experience is that of being alive as a human being, prior to accomplishing anything or fulfilling our desires. We must dare to claim the right to be here on this good earth, at this precious time. Mindfulness meditation encourages us to communicate with all aspects of our being and all aspects of experience. In order to do this we must be vulnerable, gentle, tender and open to all aspects of ourselves, the good and the bad, the ugly and the beautiful.

We have so many entrenched beliefs about our daily life. We commonly believe that funerals are supposed to be sad and weddings are supposed to be happy, that young children are supposed to be cute, cuddly and lovable, and that very old people are no longer supposed to be sexual. What we have held to be true for our entire lives may not be true in all, but only an entrenched belief.

Perhaps we notice in the midst of a funeral service that the air is crisp and that there is the fragrance of wood burning from a distant fireplace. Perhaps it's autumn and there's a beautiful display of red, gold and yellow foliage, as your loved one is being lowered into the ground, and your heart is breaking. It seems outrageous and even insulting, but you might find yourself strangely gratified that you are alive with the vibrancy of this immediate sensory moment.

We're supposed to be sad according to conventional standards, but instead we find ourselves *both* sad and also delighted, empty and also full. If we don't carry our inventory of beliefs and judgments with us, then we can have such a multidimensional experience of broken heartedness and aliveness. Losing a job is supposed to be unfortunate, and breaking up with a loved one is supposed to be terribly sad and gut wrenching. Perhaps such endings lead to a more creative job or a new beautiful life with someone else. We could discover a mixture of devastation and delight.

To allow ourselves to be touched by basic being means that we drop our map and our agenda over and over again. We drop our strongly held beliefs and open to the possibility that our life may turn out to be completely other than what we had thought. When we are not holding ourselves so tightly, we have the chance to see both ourselves and the world without wanting either to be different from the way they are. We don't always love our partners, our parents or our good friends. To hold onto such beliefs may prevent us from meeting the moment we're already in.

What if situations don't have to be anything other than what they are? Our age-old beliefs armor us against seemingly unpleasant events, which may turn out to be auspicious. Meditation suggests that it might be refreshing to approach everyday life without armor, meeting its nakedness with our own. We reach a point where we recognize that we don't have to change ourselves, our spouses, or our friends, in an attempt to make them better. The situations that we find ourselves in may be fine the way they are. This realization is radical, and may be regarded as 'crazy' by ordinary people.

The fruitional aspect of mindfulness practice is when we finally stop wanting others to be different than they actually are. This is a profound form of compassion we can offer another. This also means that we are willing to be with our neuroses and don't have to beat ourselves up for being less than perfect.

Mindfulness meditation is the paradoxical practice of *non doing*. We practice being silent and still without resistance, tension or inner conflict. There's nothing to add and nothing to subtract from our momentary experience. It is the natural state of an undisturbed mind. We do not have to fight with what arises in our mind or attempt to manipulate it in some way.

We develop *maitri* or friendliness to ourselves by not judging what arises in our experience of meditation. Without this intimate connection to ourselves we cannot appreciate our world or be of service to anyone else. Only when we establish an intimate connection with all aspects of ourselves without judgment, do we experience a sense of wholeness, a sense of being of one piece.

Chapter 3

Samsara: The Difference between Dogs and Lions

The Buddhist view of meditation is one of choiceless awareness. We don't pick and choose what we're going to be aware of. That is, we don't focus our awareness on the good stuff, and avoid the so called bad stuff. Choiceless awareness means that we allow ourselves to be open and sensitive to all of our experiences. We bring mindful awareness to as many situations in life as possible and so we learn from all things.

There is a fundamental difference between dogs and lions. When you're with a dog and you throw a stick, the dog will faithfully chase the stick. When you throw a stick before a lion, the lion will chase *you* not the stick. Like faithful dogs we have been chasing 'sticks' forever. Our mind throws out a thought and we go after it. The mind throws a memory, an image, a desire, and we eagerly chase it. Even when our mind recycles terribly painful thoughts and images, we chase them as well, re-experiencing old events with renewed anguish.

Like dogs we have been faithfully chasing all the stuff that the mind throws to us for a very long time. We have not caught on that this game is not going anywhere. There is no ultimate stick that ends the game. The mind continues to throw out an endless array of sticks and we chase them, and for most people this madness is considered normal.

The lion is not fooled by the game of sticks. It looks directly at the *thrower* of the sticks. The lion-like meditator does not chase the mind's productions, but instead looks directly at the mechanism of mind, its entire bureaucracy and how it works. When we go after the stick and identify with it, we are taken for a ride to nowhere. This is the default practice of *mindlessness* or madness. When a thought, image, memory or desire arises in the mind and we recognize it for what is, we are *disidentifying* with it, letting it go. This is the practice of mindfulness.

When we look directly at the mind itself and recognize the pointlessness of the game of chasing sticks, this is called insight or *vipashyana* in Sanskrit. It is a re-cognition, a knowing again, but from a larger perspective. In spite of such insight, due to the conditioning that we have been subject to our entire lives, initially, all we can do is catch a glimpse of this neurotic pattern. The weight of conditioning pulls us back into our habitual way of being stick chasers.

The chasing of the mind's productions is what is called **samsara** in the Buddhist tradition. Samsara is collective neurosis, marked by restlessness, impulsivity and dissatisfaction. It is the unbroken wheel of wanting what you can't get, getting what you don't want, or eventually getting who or what you thought you wanted, only to find out that you're still not completely satisfied. Samsara ranges from a vague feeling of dissatisfaction to gross suffering. Even for many well-adjusted, high functioning individuals, it is the feeling of carrying some kind of burden, perhaps an unquenchable thirst to squeeze more out of life.

Samsara is based on not trusting our mind as it is, nor the world as it is. The implication is that we all feel a sense of personal deficiency, that we're not enough. We believe that we need to protect and perpetuate our personal territory, which we hope will compensate us for this feeling of inner deficiency. Losing track of the underlying motivation behind many of our actions causes confusion both for ourselves and others.

Metaphorically, samsara is a restless animal. It is very hungry for stimulation and distraction, and it moves over the landscape of our lives stalking anything that promises to fill its emptiness. It will devour anything that catches its attention in order to expand its empire. It is hypersensitive to noises in the forest that sound like either predators or competitors for its prey, and so it growls and fluffs up its fur in order to frighten other animals away. No matter how often it feeds itself, running tirelessly after what it thinks is nourishment, it remains hungry. As many times as it wards off others, who appear threatening, it never feels entirely safe.

If you watch this animal from an aerial point of view, it cuts a zigzag path, alternately devouring what is pleasurable or chasing away what is threatening. It is both hungry and fearful. The animal of samsara is very hard to recognize because its bushy tail sweeps away its own tracks. When you try to follow it in order to see what it is doing, to observe its behavior and its eating habits, you can't find its footprints. That bushy tail is what the Buddhist tradition calls *ignorance*, the avoidance of the truth of 'what is'.

I have been describing what Buddhism calls the *three poisons*, craving, aggression and ignorance, the lubricants of the samsaric wheel. From the meditators' perspective, the poison of ignorance is the most deadly because it blinds us from recognizing how much reactive liking and disliking, pushing and pulling we are doing. The animal of samsara is hard to witness because of the blinding power of ignorance which can appear as forgetfulness, denial, inertia, or simply spacing out.

In Western psychological terms, *neurosis* could be a substitute for samsara. Neurosis also hides from itself by resorting to defense mechanisms, which block awareness of painful truths. As a result, we feel at a distance from ourselves, disconnected, and separate from our seamless totality. There's 'me' and my mind, and 'me' and my body, and 'me' and my beliefs, 'me' and my feelings, 'me' and 'my life'.

This feeling of separation causes a great deal of pain which underlies our search to always feel better. We all want to find some sort of grand remedy so that we don't have to feel so divided between our animal self and our spiritual self, between our body and our soul, between ourselves and others. Samsara is the painful experience of not feeling like one integrated being. Once we presume separation from ourselves, and separation from others, then the only way we have of relating is through like and dislike, ignorance and denial.

Everyone you see is fighting a battle that you know nothing about. As you walk the streets of your hometown or city, whomever you come across is also fighting a silent battle. Everyone experiences a vague sense of lack, a deficient emptiness or hollowness. We all carry on the necessary business of everyday life and we function in various social roles, but rarely do we recognize this battle. We are carrying an unnameable burden from which we want relief, and this is where our attention is subliminally focused.

Some of us are afraid of being abandoned and so we struggle to become indispensable to our mates, hopefully guaranteeing that they will stay in love with us. We struggle to be loved and to be cherished as a guarantee that we won't be abandoned. Others of us are very afraid of failure, afraid that we're not going to accomplish our goals and objectives. So, we constantly struggle to achieve success. We are compulsively driven towards accomplishment and achievement, ceaselessly trying to climb the mountain of success, but we are rarely at ease.

Others struggle with the secret belief that they are not intelligent. They struggle to read a lot of books, take workshops, and gain vast accumulations of knowledge. They may get extra degrees, or take a steady stream of adult education courses in order to feel knowledgeable or wise, but the shadow of personal deficiency still plagues them.

Some of us struggle with the feeling that we don't have what it takes to survive in a dog-eat-dog world. We may feel that we were not given the right stuff genetically and that we're one of the runts who's not going to thrive in the contest of life. We struggle to align ourselves with strong people and then perhaps marry them. Or we may join an organization that we feel is just and powerful which will hold the umbrella over our head and put a safety net under our feet. But we are distrustful, wondering how long such safety will remain in place.

Some of us feel that we do not possess intrinsic value, that we're insignificant, and that we don't count. We fail to respond to our own wishes and needs because we don't honor ourselves. Instead, we struggle to meet others' needs and wants as a way of earning personal worthiness. Secretly, we're waiting for someone to intuitively grasp what we need and to give it to us, hoping that someone will value and cherish us because we are unable or unwilling to do it ourselves.

I have been describing *samsara*, as it appears in the form of personality dynamics which reveals different styles of endless struggle, going in circles and not arriving where we would like. The good news is that Buddhism invites us to bring our neurotic struggle with us to the path. We bring our obsessive compulsiveness, our arrogance, our hysteria, our feeling of being poverty stricken to the meditation cushion. This is the way we all begin. We practice meditation because we have a very genuine desire to stop suffering.

If we are going to transform ourselves from dogs to lions we must allow the teachings to be very personal. It's a common mistake to relate with the dharma or teachings as an exotic import to be used as a spiritual detergent to wash ourselves clean. When we completely identify with the dharma then our mind *is* the Buddha, our life *is* the path of dharma and whomever crosses our path *is* our sangha (Buddhist community). It's that close, that intimate.

The lion looks at the mind in its nakedness and sees that it spontaneously projects thoughts, images and narratives onto the world. The lion is not fooled into thinking that the world actually contains those qualities. The lion discovers that when it doesn't feed those projections with attention, they dissolve of their own.

At that moment the lion discovers the truth of 'what is', the mind's innocence.

With this recognition comes a peacefulness that comes from knowing that there's no need for struggle, no need to grasp, reject or ignore the truth of what is. In this state our personality becomes transparent permitting our Buddha nature to shine through. By living with such intimacy we discover the sacredness of everyday life.

Chapter 4

No Alibis

Throughout the day there are continual moments of openness and possibility, but also uncertainty. Usually another thought comes to fill in the space, or we slip into a familiar social role where we go on autopilot. For the meditator, the challenge is whether we are able to just linger in the space of 'don't know' and trust what happens next.

Many of us are afraid to go there because we don't know where it might lead. You could discover that you feel like crying with joy, or maybe hugging a tree, or biting into a Macintosh apple, and surprise yourself. This is the path of the spiritual warrior without alibis.

A number of years ago a group of experimental psychologists from New York University assessed the impact of the unconscious or non-conscious mind on our everyday consciousness. The non-conscious is the dimension of mind that we are not commonly aware of, but which exerts significant influence on our everyday activities.

The experiment involved hypnotizing a willing subject, a middle-aged woman, who upon hearing the sound of the experimenter snap his fingers, would crawl on her hands and knees in the midst of a formal social occasion. At the appointed time when the cue was given, this dignified, well-dressed woman, suddenly got down on all fours and began crawling around on the carpet in the midst of a roomful of people engaged in discussion.

Within moments she spontaneously exclaimed, "I wonder where I dropped my earrings!" Finding herself crawling around the carpet on all fours, the whole situation must have felt entirely bizarre and incomprehensible to her. In order to prevent a paralyzing feeling of discontinuity from her usual sense of self, she provided herself with a plausible justification for why she was crawling on the carpet. As a result, she experienced no disruption or discontinuity from her familiar sense of herself.

The experimenters concluded that her everyday mind completely justified her bizarre behavior by manufacturing the belief that she had just lost her earrings. Her conscious mind filled in the blank of incoherence so that her *identity remained intact.*

According to Buddhist psychology most of us are doing this all the time. That is, we enact habitual behaviors and patterns of thought and feeling that fit us like a glove, that feel in alignment with our idea of ourselves. The aspect of mind that we call ego is very adept at providing rationales for why we do what we do in order to justify otherwise neurotic behavior. This is why it is so difficult to truly transform ourselves. We do not have an objective view of ourselves. We tend to live within the familiar description that we have created for who we think we are and how we think the world is.

Ego strenuously formats all of our experiences, all of our encounters with others, as well as our inner conversations, so that they are consistent with our self-concept, who we take ourselves to be. As in the case of the hypnotized woman, we unconsciously manipulate our experiences to make them reflect our sense of self, and this madness is rarely recognized for what it is.

The implications of this social experiment are worthy of consideration. In truth, moment by moment, we are confronted with the unknown. None of us knows what the next moment will bring. According to Buddhist psychology, with the arising of each moment we find ourselves momentarily uncertain and appre-hensive, but these gaps are beneath our radar. Ego deflects attention away from this gap of uncertainty and ambiguity by provoking us to make a familiar gesture.

Sitting down with a friend or intimate we might immediately make small talk to break the awkwardness of silence and to avoid the nakedness of simply looking at one another, which is so revealing.

The spinning of thoughts is a marvelous strategy for deceiving ourselves. It is similar to twirling a lit incense stick in a circular motion at night. It offers the visual illusion of an unbroken circle. Ego uses the same strategy with individual thoughts, images and feelings, creating the convincing sense of a solid and continuous entity, 'me' while reinforcing our familiar description of the world. Ego prevents us from seeing ourselves and the situation before us objectively by filling in all the gaps with our inner narrative.

These moments of uncertainty are like being in a foreign country where you don't speak the language and where you've lost both your wallet and your passport. In the Tibetan Buddhist teachings, that bare moment is called a *bardo*. This gap or interval is a wrinkle in time, between the ending of one thing and the beginning of the next. Here there are no familiar reference points to reinforce our sense of self. There are many potential possibilities in that gap, but our culture does not know what to do with this existential openness, and so we are not taught by our parents or our teachers to value this gap.

If the hypnotized woman was completely present with her experience, she would have to admit to herself that she didn't know what on earth she was doing crawling around on all fours. She might have recognized that there is more to herself than she previously imagined, aspects of herself that feel alien. That's the beginning of wisdom. Such honesty could provoke her to explore her experience further.

Mindfulness, on and off the cushion, is the practice of leaning into this edge of uncertainty and ambiguity, where we get to see the mechanics of experience directly. In the usual flow of our daily routines we do not get to objectively witness the infrastructure of what we commonly refer to as 'myself'. Buddhism teaches us that when our attention is distracted away from the experience of nowness, there is a tendency to go on automatic pilot. We insert habitual thoughts, feelings and behavior into the neutral space of nowness, and then we are reassured that we know who we are.

The history of ego is the constant effort to seek confirmation in the eyes of the world to reassure ourselves that our self-image or self-concept of ourselves is reinforced. From a meditator's point of view, the gap or the moment of nowness, holds the secret of our *egoless* identity. It reveals that we are more a field of awareness rather than a solid center *in here*.

According to developmental psychology, ego's initial intention was to create boundaries to protect the innocent and fragile mind of a child from the overpowering influences of the outside world, and the potentially disintegrating effect of its own psyche, from which the ego emerged. Ego is a strategic activity and not an actual entity. Somehow in our maturation we forgot that, and assumed instead that we were the psychic territory bounded by our own protective fence.

In moments of clarity we suspect that ego doesn't speak for our totality. Like the hypnotized woman, ego uses our life force by spinning our thoughts, images, memories and desires in a circle, creating the illusion that it is solid and continuous. If you doubt this, the next time that you're sitting quietly, doing nothing, that is, meditating, ask yourself why you are continually thinking about yourself or your life situation practically all of the time. You might discover that this self preoccupation centralizes your awareness inwards giving the reassurance that "I continue to feel like me".

The result is that we create a cocoon of safety and security, but we risk repeating ourselves without ever feeling that our life is a genuine journey. The Buddhist path inspires us to cultivate the courage of a warrior so that we are more willing to open into that naked space of nowness without overlaying it with our old patterns.

Imagine dancing with your beloved partner after having a good meal and intimate conversation. You're dancing without a trace of self-consciousness as there's no one on the sidelines watching. Everything is going swimmingly well until you situate yourself *outside* of the dancing as an observer. You comment to yourself, "My god, what a great time we're having. Look how well I'm dancing!" At that point you step on your partner's toes, as this awkward moment fractures the living energy of the moment. At this point there is you, your partner, the activity of dancing, and your judgments. When we're in the flow of an activity, then passion is not neurotic and the activity can be graceful.

The problem is that ego subjugates the natural life force, usurping its energy in order to further its own empire, the subjective inner 'me'. The result is that it disconnects us from the flow of life. Ego colonizes our experiences, separating us from the larger source of energy that is the world. In the experience of nowness, we do not stand out and apart from experience, but we're it, the entire field of experience. We are not who we think we are, and that thought is both terrifying and liberating.

In order for our spiritual path to evolve it is necessary to develop appreciation for neutral space, to actually communicate with those gaps before we go on automatic pilot. What would this look like? Can you remember a time when you paused momentarily just before you were about to bite into a peach, and suddenly inhaled its sweet fragrance or were delighted by its pastel red color? Can you remember a time when you were fully present with a loved one, as a precious moment was unfolding, and your heart opened? Can you stop the world for a moment in order to hear the melodious chirping of a bird, or delight in the cool breeze moving across your face that playfully tussles your hair?

Initially these moments can be disorienting because they break up the hypnotic flow of our habitual activities. By interrupting our continuous mind static we challenge our tired categories that frame the world into good and bad, ugly and the beautiful. By actually pausing and learning to appreciate those moments of uncertainty, we enter into intimate relationship with the always naked quality of nowness.

We could catch ourselves at any moment of the day, whether we are looking in the mirror and are about to comb our hair, whether we're trying to get out the door without forgetting to take all of our necessary belongings, or whether we are trying to get through our emails before we prepare dinner. At any one of those moments, we can just pause a second, as if to drop inside the moment, to get within its essence in order to relax into a natural state of being.

We might experience the joy of simply being alive. It is a deep appreciation for human incarnation right now, in this moment. It's the most natural thing in the world, but if our mind is spinning then there is a barrier between us and our surrounding world. Once we feel separate from the world then our relationship to it becomes strategic: either we grasp what promises pleasure, we reject what is threatening, or we ignore what does not fit into either category.

The experience of nowness offers a brightness that allows for insight and understanding, and a heat that radiates both passion and compassion. When we open to this energy without ego's manipulations it inspires us to appreciate this wonderful natural world in spite of all the terrible things occurring on the planet.

Living within this openness is unchartered. There is no map, so the quality of experience is very fresh and revealing. Our unfolding lives provide the guidance necessary for life to be a journey. Perhaps we could peer into each other's eyes without knowing what to do next, trusting that this moment is sufficient unto itself. As we learn to trust the intelligence of openness, we get glimpses of our identity with it. We can use the life force to be truly free, liberated from ego's tyranny.

Chapter 5

Spiritual Sobriety: The Three Marks of Existence

We're larger than our experience of suffering at any moment. We tend to experience so much unhappiness because we so completely identify with so-called negative states of mind. We feel enclosed within their tight boundaries and there is no room to breathe outside of them. Buddhism suggests that we are the space of awareness within which suffering is occurring and that our true dimensions extend beyond it.

One of the earliest teachings that the Buddha gave was on the *three marks of existence*. Although this is a preliminary teaching, its implications are profound and paradoxical, and it sets the foundation for the whole Buddhist path. The ideas and images that we hold about ourselves and the world determine how we live and die, suffer and rejoice. The Buddhist 'three marks' challenge us to seriously re-examine who or what we take ourselves to be so that we may begin to transform our relationship with suffering.

In this early discourse Buddha stated that all beings are 'marked' by impermanence, suffering, and egolessness. In brief, everything changes, while every being clings to some notion of permanence and therefore suffers unnecessarily, and yet paradoxically, no *one* suffers. How could this be?

On a very obvious level we know that everything is changing. We used to be 21 years of age and now we're 35 or perhaps 56. We used to be thin and shapely, and have chestnut hair, but now we may be round, soft and gray. Our children used to be cute, cuddly and dependent upon us, and now they are rebellious teenagers or overly committed adults who no longer have time for us.

The inescapable fact of change doesn't seem to sit right with us. Secretly, we all want to plant our flag down somewhere, on some territory, and claim it as our own. In so doing, we hope this territory will be immune from the maddening affair of change and contradiction. Our human wish is that at least one thing will stay the same and be protected from the ravages of change.

Our imagined oasis may be our loving marriage, our beautiful family, the home we've worked so hard to get, our livelihood, or it could be our yoga regimen, or our spiritual practice of meditation. We may think to ourselves that at least our meditation practice or our relationship with our spouse is the one thing that we can count on in the midst of the whirling sandstorm of shifting forms.

Ironically, it is our very motivation to make something safe and secure, exempt from diminishment and decay, that causes our unnecessary suffering. We may acknowledge the truth of impermanence on a conceptual level, but Buddha's enlightenment revealed that in a private corner of our mind we are fighting a life and death battle to protect the final safety of 'me' and 'mine'.

Even our relationship with ourselves changes. When we wake up in the morning we may feel burdened as we anticipate a busy day ahead. After our first cup of coffee we may feel a bit more inspired, and have a better relationship with ourselves at that point. A little later in the morning, after our third cup of coffee, we may be feeling pretty full of ourselves until we receive a phone call or an email that presents us with a problem or conflict. We might suddenly become moody, even obsessed and preoccupied because we're now burdened with one more thing on our already full plate.

The seemingly solid and continuous entity that we presume is 'I' or 'me' is not all that uniform and consistent. Our moods, feelings and thoughts fluctuate throughout the day, as does our sense of self. Impermanence happens not only on the obvious outer level, but on the inner psychological and emotional level as well.

This phenomenon is open to investigation. You don't have to believe this as an article of faith. Our everyday experience affirms the truth of impermanence which can be inspected on many levels. The entity that we call 'me', that is, our idea of ourselves, can be witnessed changing day by day, hour by hour, moment by moment. Yet, we hold onto an internal picture or image of ourselves that convinces us that we are the identical person through time and space.

One Buddhist contemplation is to examine this self-concept meticulously by looking directly at the mind to discover *who* or *what* this entity is. Hard as we may try to pinpoint a singular, unitary, consistent self, we find instead a kaleidoscope of mental snapshots that portrays ourselves in differing guises, relationships and functions, having very different experiences.

If we continue looking at our history to discover an unchanging entity, we're hard pressed to locate a permanent self that began someplace, and has remained the same individual throughout the continuity of our lived experiences. We conventionally assume that a consistent, uniform 'I' maintains its identity throughout all of our experiences, but this is seldom directly observed.

Where does 'I' exist right now? When we look at our mind to identify 'me', the part of the mind that we have located has now become an *object* for a subtle subject. If we turn our gaze on the *subject* to discover whether that is our true identity, that subject now becomes an *object* for an even more subtle observer. There's no end to this, as it leads to an infinite regression of ever more subtle subjects which cannot be observed directly without reducing them to objects.

The Buddha taught that our true identity lies in that relaxed open space of awareness that we've been fleeing from all of our life. Paradoxically, we do experience suffering, but as we look precisely at our experience with meditative awareness, we find that suffering doesn't belong to any *one*, any unchanging consistently uniform being. For instance, in the midst of emotional pain, we may experience a sequence of unpleasant sensations, but in succeeding moments we could experience hope or fear, pleasure and pain, and yet still believe that we are *only* suffering. With mindfulness we can see that each moment is a different expression of our human experience but does not reveal a continuous underlying 'me'.

Such an insight is highly paradoxical and may seem clear in one moment, and then totally obscure in the next. This paradox completely contradicts our everyday experience and this is why it is so difficult to stabilize such a realization within our personality. However, when this is realized, painful circumstances are gradually transformed into a heightened awareness of momentary sensations and feelings without neurotic struggle.

The three marks of existence suggest that our original nature is egoless, which does not mean the absence of identity. It is that sense of awareness or knowingness that is witnessing our experience right now. This awareness 'walks' with us step by step through our entire life.

The grand question is whether we would suffer if we got clear and sober about the truth of impermanence? Couldn't we just flow or harmonize with the evanescent quality of life? No matter how long we have been meditating, it is very difficult to not be attached to the security of permanence, that is, wanting our sense of self to remain solid and continuous so that our identity is assured. If we look more deeply into why we do get attached, the teachings get more subtle. We begin by examining our motivation for resisting change.

To do this inquiry properly it's best to first deeply relax and bring your attention inwards so that you can actually feel the subtle energy in your body, right now. If you can actually drop down to feel the ground level of your being, you might make a remarkable discovery. You are struggling second by second, seeking alternatives to this present moment, as if it were terribly lacking or insufficient.

This seeking is somewhat like a nervous twitch, an impulse of wanting something other than what we presently are experiencing. It is an avoidance of what the present moment is offering us. We're actually pushing, pulling, twisting and manipulating the immediacy of this ever-present moment because of a profound restlessness. This is the subtle meaning of the second mark of existence, suffering.

According to the teachings on the three marks of existence, our human suffering is caused by our refusal to embrace this always immediate moment. Even pleasurable experiences are resisted in their naked state. We tend to manipulate pleasurable experiences by trying to enhance or amplify them, or by attempting to prolong them, or as a last resort, by trying to prevent pleasurable experiences from dissipating.

The sane alternative to the madness of manipulating the always immediate moment is to begin making a relationship with neutral psychological space. The human mind appears to be terrified of neutral psychological space for it is experienced as having no meaning, no purpose, no destination. Our familiar identity is in question. When we completely let go of all tension in our mind and body, it feels like we're dissolving into formlessness, which feels like death for most people, and so we resist relaxing into it. The experience of spacious awareness is typically rejected out of fear of becoming permanently lost and so we fill in the space with distraction or entertainment.

A deeper understanding of impermanence reveals that it is an expression of what Buddhists call, 'emptiness' or shunyata in Sanskrit. Everything in the universe is interdependent, each thing or entity deriving its very existence from its relationship with a multiplicity of other things, as the science of ecology demonstrates. Nothing exists as an isolated entity. When we try to pinpoint the so-called 'me' we find an endless succession of relationships that support and give meaning to 'me', and without which 'me' can't exist.

As our spiritual practice matures we realize that the world is not just an empty canvas, a featureless landscape, but is populated by things and beings, husbands, wives and families, trees and caterpillars, waterfalls and cumulus clouds. After witnessing everything as interdependent, multidimensional, and empty of our projections, the world of form returns with brilliance. Now we might glimpse the world nakedly as a child would experience it. We see the transparency of our conceptual padding of the world, our social roles, and our conventional behavior. The world of form comes back with clarity, simplicity and nakedness.

How does all this relate with personal suffering? If we habitually misuse our mind by whirling our memories, plans, projects, regrets and misgivings, resentments and anticipated triumphs, it creates the illusion of a solid 'me' in here. The natural world can no longer pierce us to touch our heart. We're too solid. To the degree that we have shed these concentric circles of defense, the multilevel conversations going on simultaneously, only then does the world penetrate us. The natural world can feel erotic, as sight, sound, smell, taste and touch enter our systems and make lovers of us all.

We don't have to be timid about getting bruised by having the world brush up against us. We can't defend ourselves from life anyway. The positive side of vulnerability is that when we are psychologically naked then we can fall in love every day. We can feel love and compassion for the old man's sitting alone on a park bench feeding pigeons, or feel deep affection for the stray cat that rubs up against our legs, or the baby in a stroller who catches our adoring gaze and smiles back at us. Perhaps we marvel at the play of sunlight on the surface of a lake, and experience deep gratitude.

But we mustn't try to capture any experience in an effort to make personal territory out of it. We *touch* our experience with mindfulness and awareness and *let go*, thereby short-circuiting ego's ambition to expand its empire. The third mark of existence, egolessness, permits us to open to the sacred dimension of life. We let ourselves be penetrated by everyday phenomena but we let go immediately, starving ego's acquisitive hunger in the process. This is the discipline of meditation in everyday life. It is the freedom of choiceless awareness where our struggle to preserve an unchanging self-image is no longer in play and where pleasure and pain are on equal footing.

When we bring mindfulness into our daily activities we don't have to squeeze every last drop of pleasure out of situations or feel deprived when we are unable to do so. We are very manipulated by pleasure and pain, hope and fear, and ideas of gain and loss. With mindfulness we might notice that when we are not defending ourselves, life could be *both* smooth and rough, vivid and penetrating.

In moments of egoless awareness we could 'ride' situations instead of react to them. We could deal with the raw and rugged qualities of life as long as we discipline ourselves to not be endlessly seduced by pleasure or diminished by the threat of pain.

Chapter 6

Overcoming Loss of Heart: The Four Reminders

Like licking honey from a razorblade, our neurotic hunger for security and comfort offers momentary pleasure which is soon cut by the sharp edge of impermanence. As spiritual warriors we should not use meditation to seek shelter from the uncompromising realities of the human condition but walk the razor's edge as our path.

As our mindfulness practice matures it is likely that we will become less stressed and more peaceful. Yet, there are certain unavoidable challenges that come along which threaten our new found tranquility. We are all plagued by many compelling concerns: "I was terminated at work because my company is relocating; I missed a mortgage payment and I'm going to be penalized; I can't believe I sold off my stocks just before the market sky rocketed; my car didn't pass inspection and I don't have the money to fix the exhaust system."

Sometimes a cluster of these events hits us and knocks the wind out of our sails. We either stop meditating or our practice feels like a knot of preoccupation, lifeless and uneventful. All the great teachers of the various Buddhist lineages have recommended contemplation of *the four reminders* which turn our attention towards the dharma, when we become overly preoccupied or distracted. These contemplations shift our attention from a possible loss of heart back towards the path of awakening.

Contemplation is a complementary practice to mindfulness. It involves using our thinking process to deeply explore a particular theme with focused attention and intensity. Mindfulness prevents us from getting derailed so that we can take our meaningful contemplation as far as we wish. Beyond the petty irritations and periodic setbacks of everyday life, the existential issues of death, meaninglessness, aloneness and contingency confront every sensitive and conscious individual at some point.

There are occasions when we wake up in the middle of the night and are seized with the thought that our life, our work and our marriage and our relationships all feel hollow. Or we may wonder if anything that we do or experience, matters in the big scheme of things. Yet, we may wake up in the morning and feel that an aura of meaningfulness has reinstated itself, and our life resumes its normal tone and texture.

Whether we're single or married with children, have fruitful livelihood or not, whether we have established a community of close friends or feel marginalized from community, the alternation of meaning and meaninglessness may leave us with doubt and uncertainty.

The first of the four reminders recommends that we contemplate our *precious human birth* which inspires deep appreciation for the rare occasion of this life, a consideration that should not be taken lightly. Because we age day by day, which is the nature of the human condition, we are reminded to take advantage of our auspicious circumstances. We could celebrate the precious occasion of our human existence, the miracle of this life, where we can practice meditation and wake up to our full potential.

Precious human birth also means that we may be fortunate to be 'free and well favored', that our five senses permit us to mate with the natural world of sight and sound, taste and touch. We use a most complex form of written and spoken language so that when someone speaks to us, we're able to decipher those sounds and instantly make meaning of them. The contemplation of precious human birth evokes a sense of opportunity, that we could actually take advantage of this life.

All of the great teachers of the various Buddhist lineages have proclaimed the rarity of being born as a human being. They have taught that consciousness can take a billion different forms. We ourselves could have incarnated as a salamander, a three-toed sloth, a dolphin or a dog. Although such beings are perfect as they are, how remarkable that our consciousness has arisen in this human body and brain.

With our astounding cerebral cortex we can be self-reflective, fashion tools to create a civilization, and to articulate an inner map of the soul. We can harness the forces of nature and invent things the world has never seen before. We alone, among all animals on earth have the capacity to genuinely understand why we are born and what this human life is about. This first reminder counterbalances our random bouts of meaning-lessness.

Although we have the precious opportunity to be born as human beings, our situation is also precarious. We are on thin ice for death comes without warning, living as we do in an impermanent universe. How do we establish 'meaning', knowing that time will run out on us? In view of life's whimsical twists and turns, how do we prevent ourselves from falling into doubt and despair when there seems to be no rhyme or reason to many painful events? Can we find lasting refuge in our relationships with significant others or with a community of friends, given our existential aloneness?

As we get older the idea of death is no longer a concept, particularly when we reach midlife. Death signals the irrevocable end of all our intimate relationships, the termination of all our projects and ambitions, all of our wishes and fantasies. Death triggers images of the unthinkable final moment of having to say goodbye to all of it. No bargaining is possible, nor does death admit of a solution.

Most people tend to hold only a concept of death, suppressing any profound reflection upon their mortality. There's a great seduction to misuse the practice of meditation to cultivate tranquility and try to sidestep the confrontation with our necessary mortality. The second of the four reminders encourages us to *contemplate impermanence* to anchor our practice in reality. It provokes us to seriously question the distorted belief in either eternalism or nihilism, that we will either live forever or that nothing matters.

From the Buddhist point of view, death is considered the boundary of life without which life would be like a picture without a frame, a landscape without a horizon. Without impermanence life would be a still life of plastic flowers which never changes.

Without death there is no change, and without change there is no journey and no possibility of transformation. When we contemplate death we regard it as a regenerating force that permits life. Paradoxically, the boundary that is death is actually what allows us to be free. If we ignore the boundary, our so-called freedom is wishy-washy, not real freedom.

Authentic freedom means that we acknowledge and work within certain unmistakable limitations. Death is a very uncontestable limitation, indicating that we have only a certain amount of time and energy to get on with our lives. This is both inspiring and terrifying because we know that time is going to run out on us. We won't be able to complete all of our projects, or visit all of our favorite countries, or read all of the books stacked upon our shelves, or do the long retreats we vowed we would when the time was right. We won't be able to fulfill everything that we have wished for and so there is an uncompromising fierceness to death.

That frightening quality of death is what prevents us from going to sleep spiritually. We do not postpone to tomorrow what needs our attention today. The contemplation on death and impermanence provokes a healthy unrest and keeps us sharp, knowing that we don't have unlimited time. It is a reminder that we're all in the same boat, and it's not coming back to shore.

Death is the great equalizer, and this may inspire us to generate compassion for all beings, who like us, were born dying. The further reaches of this contemplation involve bringing the full power of our awareness to the experience of letting go of our body during the 'living' process of dying itself.

The existential issue of contingency is the ambiguity between freedom and its opposite, chance. We Americans like to think that we are the captain of our ship and the master of our fate, that we are free to call the shots of our own life. In spite of our regular meditation practice and our wish to steer our lives towards spiritual ends, 'shit happens', as the bumper sticker reads.

Our loved ones still get seriously sick, our jobs do get outsourced, our partners may leave us for more desirable others, and we're left devastated. We may find ourselves cornered by circumstances that we didn't choose such as having to care for aging parents, dealing with our teen's addiction, or medical bills that force us into bankruptcy.

At such times we may feel like a leaf blown beyond our control by the wind of random circumstances. We might come to the conclusion that there's no rhyme or reason to our life and be left with crippling doubt or cynicism.

The third of the four reminders is the *contemplation of karma* which addresses the theme of contingency as the following example illustrates: Imagine you're walking through one of your favorite parks with a friend and you notice that there is a chess table where a game was apparently started but not finished. You and your friend spontaneously decide to play a game of chess with the pieces just as you found them.

One way to understand karma is to reflect on the truth that we cannot change our genetics, or the racial and ethnic qualities we inherited, or the conditioning that we received from our parents. Those qualities are like the pieces that were already positioned on the chess table. *How* you play the game in the present is open, and will determine the quality of your future life. Once you sit down at the chessboard you use your intelligence, skill, your intuition to play the best game you can. You are free to move your chess pieces but only from the position in which you found them, and you are free to play but only within the boundaries of the rules of the game.

The contemplation on karmic cause and effect promotes the understanding that our experiences do not arise haphazardly, but through causes and conditions that are interdependently linked. This contemplation provides a framework to contain our doubt and confusion. It works against the disempowering feeling of victimization by circumstances beyond our control.

Like a stone dropped in a pond, every gesture of body, speech, and mind creates ripples which affect both ourselves and others. We begin to recognize that even at the level of thought, we radiate very subtle energetic ripples into a vast electromagnetic field called the world. Those thoughts tend to magnetize specific qualities or situations to ourselves, or conversely they may repel qualities or situations away from us.

This contemplation reminds us that our thoughts and beliefs, our feelings and our actions will eventually produce consequences, which may occur long after their causes. Contemplating this inspires us to assume complete responsibility for ourselves by examining ourselves every day. Most importantly, it instills a sense of benign acceptance when we experience difficult circumstances.

The contemplation on karmic cause and effect inspires us to be mindful not only for our own sake, but for others as well. We practice cultivating seeds of virtue by thinking how our thoughts, conversations and actions may bring benefit or may cause harm to others. In this sense, we actually create our world, which no longer feels chaotic and haphazard, but rather coherent and meaningful.

We are participants in a vast interconnected universe, sharing our world with countless others. We're all playing our notes in this vast orchestra, and we are both initiators and recipients of the melodies. We share the responsibility for creating our world, which is neither haphazard, nor is it always comprehensible due to the vast network of influences.

Another existential issue is the experience of loneliness and isolation. As emotionally intimate and bonded as we are with our loved ones, or as well connected as we feel with our community of friends, we cannot communicate our experiences to another exactly as we are feeling them. I can touch you, hug you, write poetry, I can share my heartfelt thoughts and feelings with you, but you will take all of that into your unique system and filter it according to your own understanding. It will be *your* experience of my experience.

Aloneness here means that we can never transmit our experience to another but only through translation. It also suggests that we are the singularly unique juncture where the world incarnates through us in an unrepeatable manner.

The existential sense of loneliness can be the absence of company or the feeling of social marginalization. At a deeper level, aloneness or loneliness also suggests that through our lifelong identification with our mind-made idea of ourselves, we have disconnected from our inherent Buddha nature and have created an abyss. We suffer a lack of deep connection with our own depths. As much as we cherish our spouses and our children, or our friends and lovers, neither can complete us. Only we can complete ourselves by bridging this gap.

The fourth reminder urges us to contemplate the *unsatisfactoriness of samsara*, the experience of wanting who or what you can't get, getting who or what you don't want, or finally getting who or what you thought you wanted only to discover that you're still hungry. This contemplation cuts through our wishful thinking, our misguided hope that we will be rescued from our loneliness by another.

Samsara is the unquenchable thirst to fill an unnameable

emptiness caused by ignoring our basic sanity or Buddha nature. It is the misguided and futile effort to mend the basic split that mysteriously separates us from both ourselves and our world. There is a perpetual hunger to reach outside of ourselves to relieve our isolation and a simultaneous reflex to retreat from others when we feel threatened or when they don't adequately mirror the image we hold of ourselves. This push and pull is exactly what lubricates the samsaric wheel.

The opposite of samsara is when there's no reactive effort to be other than who we are, or to be doing something other than what we happen to be doing, or to be elsewhere from where we presently are. We open our heart and our senses to appreciate what we already are and have. When we give up the hope of being rescued, we are finally delivered to ourselves. This counterbalances the existential pain of loneliness.

Through living, loving and losing, we will have to wrestle or contend with these unavoidable existential issues. The Buddhist tradition already anticipated these concerns 2 5 millennia ago. All the major schools of Buddhism recommend contemplation of the four reminders when we become disheartened or doubtful, when we get seduced by trivial concerns, or when we think that we can postpone living in the immediacy of nowness.

Mindfulness meditation is one of the ways that we cut through the viciousness of samsara. As practitioners we try to develop simplicity in our daily affairs, giving our full attention to what is at hand. We bother to appreciate the exquisite details of everyday activities. As a result we begin to embody a quality of sanity and dignity which radiates to other people and affects their perceptions. We shine our spirit into the world demonstrating that there is an alternative way to be that is not samsaric.

Through contemplating the four reminders we appreciate this precious human birth, recognizing that our life is a time sensitive opportunity. What befalls us as experience is neither haphazard nor decreed by a divine creator, but is an inevitable outcome of prior causes and conditions. We protect our path of meditation as our true refuge and not our ego's craving for reassurance and reinforcement, and thereby avoid becoming a meal for samsara's ravenous appetite.

Chapter 7

The Noble Eightfold Path as a Buddhist GPS

The truth of the Buddhist path means that we stop depending on others or external things to rescue us from ourselves. It is not a pre-paved highway that we uniformly follow, but an elusive 'middle way' that must be discovered, as the teachings incarnate through the individual. We have to integrate our insights and inspiration into our particular culture in historical time.

The Buddha's *Four Noble Truths* proclaim the truth of suffering, its cause, the truth of its potential cessation, and finally the path that permits us to stabilize our understanding in daily life. The fourth noble truth itself is none other than the *Noble Eightfold path*, the explanation for how we can train ourselves in the midst of everyday life.

The noble eightfold path is grouped into the three larger categories of wisdom, ethical conduct and discipline. As practitioners we train in the 'right' application of each of these areas. *Wisdom* includes right view and right intention; *ethical conduct* includes right speech, right action and right livelihood; *discipline* includes right effort, right mindfulness, and right concentration or samadhi.

The word 'right' is a translation from Sanskrit and Pali and has numerous meanings. It implies thought or action that is complete, skillful, coherent, and wise. In this context the word 'right' is not in contrast with 'wrong' for that would make it a moral injunction. Instead, we could think of 'right' as thought or action that is total, complete and wholehearted, where we bring our full presence into our acts.

The noble eightfold path is a skillful method for helping us join the dharma with our everyday life, so that our meditative insight and inspiration does not remain at the level of thought alone. 'Right view', under the category of wisdom, is a completely coherent view that involves our body, our mind, and our heart at the same time. When we bring this holistic view to the path then our life journey itself *is* the goal. In other words, *how* we walk the path is itself the goal. How we handle ourselves expresses how deeply the dharma has penetrated us.

Right view is non-theistic, which is a distinguishing feature of Buddha dharma. The implication of non-theism is that we don't believe that a cosmic entity is going to rescue us from our complications and confusions, that no one is going to do it for us, but we, ourselves. Right view maybe epitomized by the example of the Buddha who awakened by himself. He is an example of how to orient ourselves towards the path of dharma by finding our own way and waking ourselves up. Of course, we do this with the help of the teachings and with the community of practitioners.

Many of us indulge in wishful thinking that when we pay off our houses or our daughter's college tuition, then we'll be happy. Or when we finally get a divorce, or finally get married, that will make us fulfilled and happy and bring meaning into our lives.

The wisdom of right view encourages us to see that our life happens now. We're not aiming towards a future happiness or resolution. We don't expect that we're going to wake up one day and that life is going to be dramatically different, as if winning the cosmic lottery. Right view is cutting through the hope that something magical is going to happen to us.

Buddhism encourages us to see our world as totally sacred which means that we don't give up on any aspect of our lives. If we hold right view than every corner of this world and the people within it are also sacred. We don't lose faith in our own fundamental goodness and basic sanity, and understand that there is a seed of awakenment in everyone.

Following from right view is *right intention*, which is what genuinely motivates us. It inspires us to contemplate what our real desire is behind our many desires. If we did a ruthless inventory of ourselves and listed all of our desires, when we got to the very heart of our deepest desire, what would be our deepest most sincere wish in this lifetime?

Right intention is to know that and to act from that place of knowing. Then we have a basis with which we can align ourselves and we can discover whether we're in sync with our view or in contradiction with it. One of the values of the eightfold noble path is to discover whether we are walking our talk or not.

When we take refuge in the dharma as the path then our intention is guided by what promotes our path rather than by what reinforces our habitual or neurotic patterns. This does not mean that we have to retreat from society. It simply implies that we become clear about what our real intention is and conduct ourselves in harmony with it.

Right intention challenges us to inquire whether we have the conviction to stick with what is most important. Are we truly committed to waking up and being of service to others under all circumstances? This means that we don't forget our intention as we're walking with a friend, and notice an elderly woman sitting alone on a bench, looking rather forlorn. We could still be involved in our conversation with our buddy, but we take a moment to make contact, stating "What a beautiful spot you've picked! The air smells so good here at this time of day, doesn't it?"

Like a ray of light penetrating a world of darkness, the elderly woman smiles back and nods her head with appreciation. Perhaps her adult children are overly committed to their own lives and her grandchildren may be away at college. There may be no one involved in this woman's life. Loneliness is her companion. We momentarily dispel the shadow of that loneliness by shining our right intention. Then we resume our conversation with our friend and continue on our way.

Right speech which is connected with ethical conduct on the eightfold path, means having the courage to tell the truth. It implies that we're not willing to have private corners in our mind any longer. Right speech means that we're willing to be authentic with another and not simply speak from within our prescribed social role. Speaking the truth means speaking from the heart and not just filling in the space to keep the momentum of a conversation going.

Telling the truth however does not mean hurting others with a blunt statement, although truthful. Our primary commitment is always to doing no harm. Telling the truth to another should be skillful communication, timely and appropriate, meant to help, clarify or inspire. It is only as a last resort, when someone is being highly indulgent or destructive, that we attempt to wake them up by speaking a direct truth.

The implication of right speech is that before we open our mouths, we also feel the space between ourselves and another person. We intuitively tune into the psychological or energetic atmosphere of the social situation. As we walk into a social occasion we might notice that something serious and emotionally heavy has just transpired. At that moment it may not be best to tell a lighthearted or goofy joke just to break the ice. We could just allow space and simply be present in a sensitive and feeling way. This is also a form of communication.

Right speech also means right silence. We know how to pause and wait for some nonverbal cue from the other person before we continue speaking. Silence becomes the background of right speech, but is not in opposition to speaking. We punctuate our conversation with periodic pauses allowing space for the other to think about what we've said or for both of us to simply be together without making a conversation happen.

Right speech could also be understood as an internal discipline as well as an interpersonal practice. We dispel the private divisions in our mind by speaking truthfully to ourselves. When we're about to do something that is in contradiction with our dharma path, we don't manipulate our inner conversation as a camouflage.

Neurosis is when we make private deals within ourselves, giving ourselves permission to cross a line to enact a familiar pattern, while ignoring that we just compromised ourselves. The practice of right speech internally, means that we shine a light on ourselves at that moment, which is very inconvenient and irritating. We give up the practice of breaking our own agreements with ourselves.

Right action follows from the integration of right view, intention and right speech. Right action must follow from the integration of our right view, intention and speech. It is knowing how to cut through the perilous seductions on the path of everyday life by not permitting ourselves to be seduced by the bandits of hope and fear, which rob us of our balance or equanimity.

Life as it is conventionally lived alternates between hoping we'll get who or what we want, but fearing that we won't. It is hoping for recognition of our unique worth, but fearing that we will remain unacknowledged and insignificant. It is hoping to always gain advantage from situations, but fearing that we will miss such opportunities. Hope and fear are the lubricants that spin the samsara wheel of collective neurosis.

We remind ourselves that we're in this world primarily to wake up and not to promote the comfort of our cocoons. Our right action flows from the intention to be of service to all others. Wherever we find ourselves, no matter what the circumstances, we can make a positive difference by being of benefit to others.

The last practice under the heading of ethical conduct is *right livelihood*. At the time of the Buddha in sixth-century BCE India, right livelihood meant not working in any industry that traps and slaughters animals, or any industry that produces weapons. In the 21st century the idea of right livelihood is considerably more complicated due to the phenomena of globalization. We're never quite sure of the negative impact of our livelihood upon the lives of others or the environment.

Perhaps one way to think about right livelihood in the 21st century is to make sure that what we do for livelihood is not in ethical contradiction with our path of dharma. This could take the form of ensuring that the company or firm we work for is involved in sustainable products and services, and that it does not exploit human beings for their cheap labor nor extract natural resources without replenishing the earth.

Another application of right livelihood might mean that wherever we happen to be working, we bring mindfulness to our workplace. Livelihood can be a profound test of our integration of the dharma with life. Whatever work we do, we often come face to face with people who are more forceful, more verbal, or more competitive than ourselves.

We often have to deal with our colleagues' aggression, territoriality and ambition, as well as with power hierarchies within our company or corporation. This could trigger our own aggression and defensiveness which now becomes a challenge for how skillfully we can handle our issues around power and competition. We don't need a monastery to effectively walk the path of dharma. Being in this ordinary world is a very good place to cultivate the discipline of the noble eightfold path.

Right effort is one of three practices under the larger category of discipline. Most of us probably apply a good deal of effort to things that either matter most to us or things with which we are preoccupied. At the same time, there are many things in life that are important which we disregard and to which we fail to apply equal effort. Usually our effort is not even throughout the day, but tends to ebb and flow.

The Buddhist path is essentially a journey without a specific goal. Every step along the way *is* the goal. Right effort implies that our path evolves one step at a time, with an attitude of appreciation and inquisitiveness with each step. We try to apply effort mixed with relaxation all throughout the day so that there is pause for refreshment. We don't push extraordinarily hard to make something happen and then have to pour ourselves a drink to take the edge off of our stress.

The practice of right effort will need to be adapted to the unique life circumstances and particular livelihood in which we are engaged. There will always be cycles of greater and lesser effort. The main point is whether or not we are overly identified and consumed with certain areas of our life which siphon all of our energy and create imbalance in ourselves, our health, and our relationships.

Neurotic effort is that kind of up and down, on and off quality, while right effort is gentle effort spread evenly throughout the day. Even when we get thrown a curve ball, we don't fall off of our seat. Whether we win the lottery or our toilet overflows, right effort reminds us that we don't need to get overwhelmed or deliriously euphoric. This evenness of effort is only possible when we view our lives and our world as sacred. Every aspect of our lives is worthy of our attention and our appreciation.

The second practice under the heading of discipline is *right mindfulness* or meditation. This does not refer exclusively to the sitting practice of meditation, but rather to how we apply mindfulness and inquisitiveness to the activities of daily life. Taking time to prepare a well-balanced dinner that is also visually appealing is as important as how we do our job or how we express love to our intimate other. Scrubbing the bathtub, polishing our Japanese table or watering our plants, as well as how we respond to a telemarketer's irritating call in the middle of dinner, are all expressions of our mindful presence or absence. Ordinary life can be the best meditator's cave or cloistered monastery.

Right mindfulness means that we remember to establish a

sense of presence and openness all throughout the day even with mundane activities such as paying bills, answering emails, dealing with ill children or animal companions. We can count on randomly getting what we don't want, or urgently wanting who or what we can't get. Right meditation is remembering to give primacy to our state of mind during such unsatisfactory occasions.

Practicing mindfulness in action is how we defeat a thousand enemies, a thousand times a day, single handedly. Dissolving the boundaries between meditation and everyday life is the basic point of the whole Buddhist path. Even when situations get the best of us, as when we slam the phone down in irritation, or raise our voice to our children, the intensity of our negative judgment and anger are potent reminders to get back on the path. Nothing is lost when we use falling off the path to get back onto the path. We can practice this all throughout the day, as best as we can.

Right mindfulness is also recognizing that we continually make up stories, positive and negative, about almost everything in life. We project our personal narrative onto others, dressing them up with our own preconceptions, expectations and demands, and then unconsciously react to our own projections. We could walk into a room and make up a whole narrative about a person who we do not know, and not recognize that we have trapped him or her in our net of assumptions and prejudices. This is the practice of madness or mindlessness.

Right mindfulness means that when we catch ourselves spinning our narrative about another, we come back to *nowness*, the naked situation of who or what is there before we dressed them up. Our new momentary perception can be refreshing and may invite us into intimate connection with our everyday world.

The last category of discipline is *right samadhi*, a Sanskrit term which means one-pointed concentration. Samadhi is the ability to stay focused without allowing distraction to sabotage our concentration. When we contemplate some aspect of the dharma, such as the four noble truths, or the phenomenon of projecting our narrative onto others, we engage our mind in a concentrated manner. Right Samadhi is like throwing a rock into the ocean, where our inquisitiveness goes all the way down until we feel that we've hit bottom, and have really understood something.

Meditation is analogous to a microscope which looks at the many elements and dimensions of mind. Samadhi is the sustained effort to continue looking with inquisitiveness without allowing ourselves to get distracted. Without that sustained looking, we don't truly penetrate the many layers of mind. Without samadhi we are unable to squeeze the secret meaning from the teachings. The inner meaning of the dharma comes from a very deep state of mind where we understand the Buddha's truths on a level that words can't convey.

The eightfold path can be thought of as a spiral, rather than a linear path of development. As our path evolves, our understanding of ethical conduct, wisdom and discipline also evolve, bringing a deepening realization to each of the noble eight limbs. Each of these categories simultaneously provides guidance but also challenges us to develop ourselves. Through study and contemplation of the noble eightfold path we plant dharmic seeds within ourselves, which are reflected in the quality of our everyday life situations and relationships.

Chapter 8

Mindfulness in Everyday Life

When we get emotionally wounded it creates a kinesthetic memory. Although the event is long past it remains psychoactive, somewhat like a phantom limb. Even though the limb has been amputated, we still feel pain where the limb was located. The kinesthetic memory can get triggered when a situation presents itself that contains similar features to the original wound. Meditation must take stock of this psychological reality and include it within its scope.

Over time the practice of meditation must include the activities of everyday life, or else meditation becomes an isolated ritual activity, at odds with our ordinary affairs. As our meditation practice matures we should notice an increasing ability to handle our life with greater sensitivity and creativity.

There are many meditators who have been meditating for many years, but who are out of touch with their bodies. Their evolution on the path is not symmetrical, in that they have developed their cognitive capacities far beyond their willingness to experience their feelings. We need to work with our emotions in a more creative manner, so that we can actually feel the living quality of their power, which allows them to become a source of insight and understanding.

There's an old story about a poisonous tree that grew in a particular village. One group of villagers decided to cut down the tree to prevent anyone from getting poisoned. They saw the world sharply divided between good and bad, and safe and dangerous, and from this perspective, they 'renounced' the toxic tree by eliminating it.

Another group of villagers was more evolved in their understanding, and feeling compassion for this living entity, decided to put a fence around the tree. The tree was still viewed as dangerous because of its poison and was kept segregated. Wanting protection from its toxicity they developed medicinal antidotes to counterbalance the painful symptoms of individuals who did get contaminated.

A third group of villagers was the most evolved in their understanding. They removed the fence and actually used the poisonous leaves and berries to make potent medicines to enhance the quality of their lives. Holding a sacred view of life they intuitively understood that embedded within the toxin was something pure and of value. Going into the essence of the toxin they were able to transmute poison into a life-enhancing elixir.

As practitioners of meditation we usually regard ourselves as a work in progress towards the goal of enlightenment. It is common to relate with our dharma path as an effort to get free from the poison of our own neurotic patterns. This is somewhat like the first group of villagers who cut down the poisonous tree in order to be protected from contagion. On the other hand, we may try to substitute peacefulness and equanimity for an upsurge of our anger, or try to substitute the feeling of generosity when we feel stingy. This is like the second group of villagers who put a fence around the tree and used various remedies as a spiritual detergent to cleanse themselves from contamination.

The most seasoned practitioners dare to make a direct relationship with so-called toxic emotions by becoming intimate with what most practitioners reject. This is analogous to the third group of villagers who used the poisonous leaves and berries as medicine to enhance their lives.

In the foundational aspect of the Buddhist path, we try to stay clear of anything toxic by drawing a line between samsara and nirvana. We try not to get polluted by negative emotions. In the Mahayana stage of the path we apply antidotes which counterbalance the poison of conflicting emotions. If we feel stingy, we practice generosity; if we feel jumpy, anxious and reactive, we practice patience; if we feel resentful we practice gratitude. These are ways of counterbalancing problematic mind states and disturbing emotions. In the Vajrayana stage we use the substance and energy of the poison itself, transmuting it into medicine to nourish our spiritual journey.

We tend to have a very confused relationship with our emotions because we're afraid they're going to overtake us. If we're experiencing pain for instance, emotional or physical pain, we usually have our guard up because we don't know how far the pain will go. We might wonder if we will lose our center of command, and so we're already in a state of fear and self-protectiveness. Although it is plausible to protect ourselves from pain, with such a defensive state of mind we are not making deep contact with our feelings.

Most of us are at war with our feelings, so that when anger, lust, jealousy, or sadness arise, it feels like it's 'us' against 'them'. There is an adversarial relationship in play and we want to control or fix these distressful feelings. But in our effort to control our distressful feelings we tend to suppress them, causing their energy to get trapped somewhere in our body. When we avoid relating with our distressful feelings we are actually *abandoning* those parts of ourselves that we find distasteful.

We could sit with such feelings and allow them to arise. Mindfulness cuts through the storyline associated with such feelings enabling us to make deep contact with the energetic life of the emotion without dramatizing it or explaining it away. The Vajrayana approach is like homeopathy, in that we take a little bit of the poison in order to correct an imbalance. We dare to open to raw emotions and use their energy wisely. This is somewhat like wading into a turbulent stream, where we let go into the current and simultaneously steer ourselves away from sharp rocks and gradually into more tranquil waters.

For instance, while at a Christmas party, and after having a couple of drinks you may find yourself in a cheerful and celebratory mood. The host of the party wants to introduce you to a good friend of hers. After a short conversation you sense that this athletic and trim individual is apparently more accomplished and successful than you are and his or her spouse is equally stunning and successful. You suddenly find yourself in a foul mood, feeling diminished and irked by a perverse wish to tarnish this couple's winning image.

If you were to analyze this situation you might temporarily pacify your mood and gain some insight and understanding, but your insecurity could linger. You would not undo the problem. The pattern that got provoked will happen again and again to you, because the complication exists within an ancient pattern of feeling. It is through opening up to your turbulent feelings and permitting it to communicate its truth that you begin to understand something about the fragility of your self-image, and how this is directly connected to your emotional reactivity.

You may also re-experience the identical feeling that you suffered, growing up with your older brother. By staying with the feeling as it goes deeper, you may recall that your brother was a straight A student and a great athlete, and that you constantly compared yourself to him. You learned to devalue yourself in comparison with him, but then began to compare and evaluate yourself with everyone else, always feeling slightly diminished by others' perceived accomplishments.

At the Christmas party you got triggered and went down the rabbit hole and wound up feeling six years old again. How do you logically reason as a forty-eight-year old with your inner six-year-old? You don't. Instead, by bringing your full attention to the actual energy of your negativity and moving with its currents, you learn to trust that it has something to communicate to you.

By dropping our storyline and immediately bringing attention to our body's sensations, we can *metabolize* the energy of the emotion by being with it and feeling it deeply, without necessarily having insight or understanding. We might learn to ride the currents of the emotion without struggle, surrendering the barrier between us and the energetic aspect of the emotion.

We tend to dissociate from the unpleasantness of strong feelings, but thereby deprive ourselves of the potential wisdom that comes from such vivid feelings. We lose our connection with the earth and live in the sky realm of the mind, where we either obsessively loop, thinking the same thoughts repeatedly, or we try to rationalize our negative feelings by justifying our negativity. "He was such an arrogant, puffed up individual and that phony smug self-assurance...."

We often create a double bind for ourselves by then judging ourselves for feeling anger, envy, sadness or vulnerability. We create double negativity, in that we're so angry at ourselves for being angry, or so ashamed of ourselves for feeling weak and frightened, that we sabotage our capacity to intimately experience our emotions.

If we're going to make medicine out of poison we must cut through the judgment immediately, and bring our full attention to the feeling itself. We then give ourselves permission to open to the energy of that feeling, using the mindfulness to cut through our personal narratives. Eventually we dissolve the barrier between ourselves and our feelings, between our mind and our body, between our body and the body of the world.

The instruction for communicating with our feelings applies to our experience of the sensory world of sight and sound, smell, taste, and touch. When a spring thundershower lashes rain against our windows, this is an invitation to simply be with it. We discover *ourselves* at the juncture of sound and our feeling of delight. The so-called outside world calls us forth to meet it through our own sensations and feelings.

When we savor a delicious dinner of sweet basil chicken we are brought into presence by what is *other* than us. This succulent dinner is none other than our gustatory awareness of this dinner. The sound of the crashing surf is none other than our vivid awareness of the crash surf.

An interesting practice is to remain sitting still after doing a session of formal mindfulness meditation. Do not meditate as you usually do. In other words, don't use the body or breath as methods of anchoring your attention and do not close your eyes as you do in your regular practice of meditation. Instead, simply be there and relax into that simple sense of presence without ambition or goal without trying to be anywhere other than where you are. At the same time, don't permit yourself to feast on rambling thoughts or space out into endless free associations.

You may notice that thoughts still occur, but they have become momentary flashings in the *background* rather than the foreground of your mind. Continue to relax in that crisp and alert sense of nowness for five to ten minutes. Afterwards, inquire whether there was a difference between this open-eyed, non directive experience and the practice of sitting mindfulness meditation. Usually, meditators are surprised to discover that aside from the difference in method that they were equally present in both instances.

This quality of spontaneous presence is your option at any moment of the day. You can be at work, or you can be driving your car on the freeway, or sitting in an office waiting to be seen by your doctor or banker, and you could just flash on that abstract sense of openness with no name, no concept, and no map. You are awake, aware and present but there's nothing to know or figure out.

You may be ambling along a street in your town or city when your mind momentarily stops and you just hear the sound of wind blowing through a pine tree. There's nothing but that perception, not even you standing apart as a witness. In the midst of an ordinary conversation you notice that your friend's face suddenly appears remarkably vivid, as you are seeing him or her objectively, beyond your mental picture of this individual.

Such brilliant perceptions are an outgrowth of regular meditation practice and occur in the overlooked slices between everyday events. One of the golden cords that runs through all Buddhist meditation is the method of abruptly cutting through our mind static and connecting with this immediate living moment.

There are endless occasions of our awareness getting accentuated by ordinary phenomena which dissolve the boundary between self and not self. The further reaches of meditation deliver us to a sacred world from which nothing is excluded. Without the ordinary stuff of our daily life with all of its complications and irritations, there is no dharma path of spiritual practice.

Chapter 9

Karma: Entrapment and Liberation

The Buddha taught that our thoughts manifest as words, and they in turn, manifest as behaviors, which develop into habits, and habits eventually harden into character or personality. We might add that character is 'destiny' in that the compelling power of our habitual patterns shape our lives in conformity with who we take ourselves to be.

The doctrine of karma is very subtle and complex. Perhaps a brief re-telling of the timeless story in Genesis might be helpful. We're told that our primal ancestors, Adam and Eve, lived in perfect harmony and attunement in the Garden of Eden. Fully woven into the fabric of their surroundings, there was no need for them to make decisions, no need to ponder options or experiential possibilities because they did not yet have a sense of being separate and distinct entities, standing apart from the surrounding environment.

Their moment by moment experience was full, complete and abundant and without any trace of lack, except of course, that they were without self-reflection. When Eve and then Adam ate from the tree of the knowledge of good and evil, they abruptly entered the world of self and other, like and dislike, pleasure and pain. They gained the capacity to conceptualize their experience, but lost their child-like innocence and were exiled from paradise. Standing out and apart from nature, from each other, and even from themselves, they now experienced shame, sorrow and alien-ation. This was the birth of time, individuality, choice and its consequences.

Interestingly, in this biblical narrative, God immediately appoints a cherub to stand guard at the entrance of Eden with a flaming sword, should the primal pair dare to return and eat of the tree of eternal life. God forbids that they should become as gods (enlightened)!

The exile from Eden was a necessary development in our evolution as a species. We needed to cut our umbilical connection with Mother Nature and develop an ego-self so that we could be self-reflective and be free to make choices. The development of the ego-self was only an intermediary step in a larger evolutionary arc.

To bring full conscious awareness into the world is to transcend the limited ego and to return to *being*, our essential awakened identity. This is the meaning of the term, Buddha. It is none other than eating from the tree of eternal life, the experience of nowness, free of past, present and future.

At this very moment, we have the potential to be 'at one' with our experiences. To be 'at one' means to fully embrace our immediate situation without resistance or manipulation to make it other than what it is. According to Buddhism, this undivided mode of experience is an expression of openness and natural intelligence. When we are in alignment with our experience and not in opposition to it, the current of life flows between us and our surroundings in sympathetic patterns of interaction.

However, there is a secondary reflex to stand outside of experience as an observer, as a separate entity, an 'I'. As with Adam and Eve's exile from Paradise, we divide in *thought* what is undivided in the natural world, as nature has no categories or neatly defined compartments.

We separate from the unbroken circle of complete experience to create a sense of 'me-ness', but in the process we exile ourselves from our true home. Once we fracture the undivided circle of experience into parts, into an experience and an experiencer, the circle begins to spin as we use sensations, feelings, perceptions, judgments and discursive thoughts to shore up the sensation of an independent 'me'. This is the ego-self which stands outside of experience as a witness.

Our increasing identification with our ego allowed us to liberate ourselves from embeddedness in nature and to individuate from the ocean of our collective psyche. Although a necessary step in our evolution as a species, the birth and development of ego marked our alienation from *being* itself, our inherent Buddha nature.

Once we separate from our essential nature we inadvertently create an internal abyss. Samsara or collective neurosis is a symptom of our disconnection from our primordial nature and our confused search to recover it in all the wrong places.

Because of this basic split we live with a profound distrust that we're not going to be taken care of unless we approach the world strategically. This in turn causes us to engage in all kinds of manipulative behaviors to get our needs met. Identified with our self-concept or ego, we struggle with ambivalence, seeking to return home to undivided, unbounded experience, yet driven to maintain our separate, independent existence.

At the core of every personality is a conflict. The ego-self is an expression both of the loss of being and the simultaneous search for it. Every personality searches for a *substitution* rather than the real article because to surrender to unbounded experience is to sacrifice the 'witness', the separate ego-self, which we're holding on to for dear life.

There is a crucial difference between the *ego image* and the *'ego functions'*. According to Western analytic psychology the 'ego functions' have to do with our ability to think, feel, and act in a coherent manner. They include the ability to distinguish between reality and imagination, the capacity to establish meaningful relationships, to predict the consequences of our actions, to control our impulses and focus our attention, and the ability to synthesize new information.

These ego functions organize and unify the other functions within the personality to insure survival, adaptation and growth.

The final outcome is the organization of these functions into an integrated psychological 'structure'. From this arises the *idea* of 'me' or 'I', our *self-image* which gives us a sense of identity. Who we take ourselves to be is actually an internalized image composed of selective memories, a self-representation but *not* the whole integrated being that we are.

The problem is that these functions are hijacked by the ego-self and used to promote its *own* survival and growth and not the organism's. Our complete identification with the ego-image becomes a denial of our soulful depth or Buddha nature. Ego strategically co-opts our organisms' survival intelligence to protect and perpetuate itself. Identified as an ego we have created a seemingly unbridgeable gulf between ourselves and the world.

At our core each of us has a deep motivation, a primary desire to feel whole, complete, and unified with experience. It is the organismic wish to function spontaneously as an integrated human being, acting in accord with our own internal design, unobstructed by our thinking, without self-consciousness.

Such spontaneity comes from a condition of egolessness, the experience of wholeness where all the distinctions and divisions within ourselves disappear. It is like playing a musical instrument or dancing without thinking what we're doing. When all of our psychological parts are united seamlessly, then we act spontaneously and are moved from a place of deeper sympathy with our environment.

Secondary motivation comes from a place of deficiency. It is a camouflage for the primary motivation of undivided experience. Examples of secondary motivations are trying to be beyond criticism because you feel that something is wrong with yourself. Or it may take the form of always trying to feel needed and appreciated because you feel you are not being loved or properly cared for. The 'all American' personality type is motivated to always be successful and accomplished because these competitive types may feel hollow inside unless they have achieved something. Yet another personality type is always trying to blend with others' wishes to promote peace because of feeling that he or she is insignificant and that one's wishes don't count.

The question of motivation is essential to an understanding of karma. Karma teaches us that both self and world are created by causes and effects, actions and reactions. The term *karma* comes from the Sanskrit root, *kr*, which means volitional or intentional action based on the idea of a self, an individual self. As already mentioned, the ego-self feels disconnected from its depths, from its innermost essence. Consequently, its desires are based on a nagging sense of deficiency, incompleteness and emptiness. Ego seeks to remedy this problem while simultaneously trying to preserve itself, the very source of the problem!

The most conventional way that humans attempt to fill in their painful emptiness is with money, food or substance, and sexual release. Based on this motivation, any one of these can become an addiction because you can never get enough of what you don't truly need.

Buddhist psychology holds that every thought, word and action that is motivated by the sense of being a separate self, leaves a psychic trace or seed in our mind. The implication is that experience prompted by *deficiency desire* leaves a trace. Because every seed seeks completion, closure, and wholeness, every seed will reach fruition at some undetermined time when the conditions are suitable. By contrast, complete experience, not enticed by a secondary or substitute desire, burns everything to ash, leaving no trace of a separate self or of a situation that needs further thought.

The practice of mindfulness meditation sees the transparency of ego's game and helps us to recognize how our self-image is an icon or symbol for our totality or Buddha nature. As we gradually make ego transparent, we intuitively sense what transcends our inner 'talking box', awareness without internal dialogue.

According to the doctrine of karma, even positive karmic seeds are not free from the lingering sense of incompletion. Positive seeds promote more auspicious circumstances to practice and evolve our spiritual path so that we may have more experience of the formless dimension within us, our Buddha nature. This most essential nature is not subject to karma because it experiences no deficiency and so it is not motivated to resolve a problem or conflict as an independent agent.

Mindfulness allows us to be more accepting of where we find ourselves. As we witness ego's bureaucracy, we have less motivation to 'improve' ourselves because of our benevolent acceptance of our present situation. This is precisely what cuts through karmic causation. In order to genuinely transform ourselves we must first accept who we are, how we are, and where we are and not impulsively seek alternatives to our present condition. Feeling into and being with our immediate circumstance returns us to wholeness, experience without division.

The fruition of mindfulness practice is the cultivation of acceptance, openness and gratitude for our present experience. We don't give into ego's feeling of deficiency and abandonment that the world is not taking care of us. We understand that we have previously planted karmic seeds, based on a sense of personal incompletion and dissatisfaction, and with an impulse to seek a remedy. We did not recognize what we were doing. Now we take ownership of our experiences and challenge ego's doubt and mistrust, and its intolerance to *presence*, to being here, now.

As practitioners of Buddhist meditation, we remind ourselves that we are at the intersection of our own and others' karmic seeds coming to fruition. We don't take samsara personally. Every thought, word and action on the part of countless others sets in motion energetic ripples, reverberations and echoes that are beyond our comprehension.

Knowing this we can practice acceptance and openness, instead of resorting to blame, complaint, regret or resentment. When we recognize situations as being beyond fault, then we can express gratitude.

We can be aware whether or not our present motivation is to cultivate the safety and security of our ego, or to protect our path of mindfulness. These are the two major forks in the dharma journey. To one side is the samsaric alternative of thirsting for what we don't yet possess, hoping for an alternative to this present moment, yearning to be elsewhere.

To the other side is the dharmic path leading to the appreciation of 'what is', experience undivided by our inner witness who judges, interprets, and endlessly comments upon everything, alienating us from this living moment. The choice is either mindfulness or madness, sanity or unending seeking and discontent.

Chapter 10

Cultural Factors Shaping Buddha's Message

Every culture through which Buddhism radiated its wisdom shaped the enlightened one's message to the mentality of its populace, and by doing so, offered novel and fresh opportunities for his dharma to shine through. In the present cross fertilization of East and West, contemporary Western culture and the ancient tradition of Buddhism are shining a light on each other's blind spot. Something very unique in the history of spirituality is being born.

Before the Buddha uttered the first word of this teaching, there was already a sacred culture in sixth-century BCE India that was in existence for thousands of years. For Indians living at that time, the world was already sacred, and the body was regarded as a temple that housed spirit. To this day when Indians greet each other they clasp their hands together at their heart, saying 'namaste' which means, "I bow to the divine spirit within you."

In ancient India space was not experienced as empty, but replete with gods and goddesses. Time was not a linear progression marked by material progress, but viewed cyclically much like the four seasons. Geographical place was not just the neutral backdrop upon which to construct a civilization, but 'place' was experienced as a unique configuration of mountains, streams, lakes and forests, and included the pattern of the winds and the particular animals that habituated a specific landscape, giving 'place' a distinctive character with its own special vibration.

Ladies and gentlemen, we're no longer in ancient India. As we fast forward 2600 years from Buddha's era to the present time, we arrive in the postmodern 21st century. As we listen to these ancient teachings of the Buddha, we might reflect upon how different we are from the early practitioners of Buddhism, and how radically different our culture is from the various Asian cultures within which Buddhism took root.

As Buddhism is being transplanted in soil thousands of years and miles removed from its source, it creates an intriguing paradox. On the one hand, the practice of mindfulness meditation opens us up to direct experience of our mind, which transcends history and culture. On the other hand, such personal experience cannot be divorced from the culturally specific forms through which it is experienced. These forms must be understood as 'pointers' to ineffable experience, but also honored, or else personal experience loses its social and cultural context.

The Buddha's teachings will, by necessity, be filtered through the lens of our culture in historical time and geographical place. If we turn our gaze on these cultural factors and make them as transparent as possible, this will prevent us from confusing the form of the teachings with their timeless spirit.

Beginning in the 20th century the teachings of the Buddha have been mingling with the unique mentality and idiosyncrasies of our Western culture, with both our psychological sophistication and our materialistic orientation, our rugged individualism and our Promethean restlessness. Something very interesting is coming out of this brew. We should be aware of what our cultural history has transmitted to us, for it has shaped our view of the world and how we relate with our spiritual path.

We live in a culture that has been highly shaped by the god-centered theistic traditions of Judaism and Christianity. Many of us are left with a hangover of sin and guilt, and doubt about our intrinsic goodness. The teaching that all sentient beings possess Buddha nature is both hopeful but also extremely challenging for Westerners to embrace. This fundamental view remains largely conceptual and not experiential, as many Buddhist practitioners still struggle with issues around self-worth and self-doubt.

In the theistic traditions as taught institutionally, God is immaterially situated in a transcendent abode, and we humans are rooted materially here on earth. At best, we can *dialogue* with the deity through prayer and establish a relationship, and we can perform good works to 'earn' divine favor, but we never can be *as* God, that is, enlightened.

By contrast, Buddha was not a god, but a spiritually awakened being who revealed a body of methods for how we also may realize that our essential nature is no different from his. This presents a radically different paradigm, as we struggle to align ourselves with our fundamental goodness and luminous awakened nature.

Paradoxically, this realization becomes possible to the degree that the self that we have taken ourselves to be, is not in the way! This creates a stunning bind for Westerners as we try to be *who* we ultimately are by not identifying with what we've imagined ourselves to be.

In contrast with the Buddhist message which affirms the preciousness of our human birth and our original enlightened nature, are psychological and socio-economic forces working in exact opposition. Several developments in our cultural history have dramatically shaped our view of ourselves, displacing us from cosmic significance and eventually led to a mood of nihilistic doubt about our fundamental goodness.

In the 19th century Darwin and his theory of natural selection proclaimed that we were an evolutionary link in a biological chain and not God's noble creation. Accordingly, our distinctively human consciousness emerged through random combinations and permutations of genetic matter and not by virtue of divine decree.

Sigmund Freud shocked the Western world with his pronouncement of an unconscious mind that shaped our thoughts, feelings and behaviors. Human reason was now precariously poised on the surface of the primordial Id, which itself was a bull pen of sexual and aggressive instincts. We were no longer masters of our own house, nor did the universe seem to revolve around us. God or spirit, according to Freud, was nothing more than an infantile projection of our longing for the great father.

Karl Marx furthered our sense of displacement and disenchantment with his revelation that class struggle and the quest for power and control, is the underlying determinant of consciousness and history. Again, our noble image of ourselves as participants in an unfolding divine drama was undermined and the belief that we were captains of our ship and masters of our fate was deflated. Darwin, Freud and Marx majorly contributed to the pervasive belief that our human awareness is shaped by unconscious, instinctual and socio-economic forces, and led to significant doubt about an indwelling spirit or soul, or an inner dimension that transcended thought.

Our culture has also been shaped by the Protestant work ethic which emphasizes hard work, self-reliance, and individual will as a sign of salvation. This led to the belief that material wealth and social status merited divine grace for the self-made individual.

Historically, the valorizing of these qualities laid the necessary foundation for capitalism, which has profoundly affected the way we live and relate with each other. Due to the capitalistic paradigm and its view of the economic marketplace as primary, every aspect of our lives has become quantified and monetized. Capitalism holds the uninspected belief in the myth of endless progress and applauds rugged individualism, competition and unrestrained economic growth.

Our human relationships have been radically shaped by capitalism's right arm, advertising. The whole industry of advertising focuses entirely on *image* rather than depth, surface appeal to elicit desire, rather than meaningful images to provoke deep feelings. We have been conditioned to be more interested in tantalizing things than in depth of experience or intimacy in relationship. We are bombarded by electronic images that associate happiness and the 'good life' with worldly success and material wealth rather than with a purpose-driven life.

Advertising has created *super* samsara, as it cultivates obsessive desire for things that we don't truly need, consumer goods and services that don't touch our soul and which leave us empty. Yet, advertising seduces us into believing that we must possess things to make us happy. Implicit in its message is that we're not OK as we are.

The unanticipated effect of this socio-cultural paradigm has been to radically shape our sense of time, so that we find ourselves always on our way towards some destination. We always seem to be on the go, filling in all the spaces with activity, and rarely do we pause to simply abide in stillness and silence. We unavoidably bring this accelerated, goal oriented mentality into our relationship with the Buddha's dharma and our practice of meditation. For many individuals, sitting still in silence goes against the grain of their conditioned hunger for stimulation and distraction, the hope for a more gratifying moment than the one they're currently experiencing.

Yet, the very same societal system that I've been critiquing may also shine a light in the dark areas of the ancient tradition of Buddhism, making explicit what has been only implicit in its doctrines. Our culture is contributing a novel perceptual frame that is more relevant to postmodern times through which we Westerners can 'get' the dharma. Our emphasis on the primacy of the individual lends a personal face to the more universal Buddha nature. We in the West will have to reconcile the paradox of the Buddhist no-self doctrine with our fierce belief in the individual personality.

Meditation is a practice of dis-identifying with our thoughts, feelings, images, memories, hopes and fears, in the service of letting go of non productive thinking and our identification with our created self-image. Meditation could be misused to avoid or deny painful areas of ourselves, and could further suppress what needs dialogue and understanding. The potential danger of the teaching on egolessness for Westerners, especially women, is the tendency to sacrifice their own inner voice and their identities by merging with their significant others and their families.

With the advantage of Western psychology's understanding of psycho-social development, its insight into repression and the creation of a shadow personality, we now understand that 'unfinished business' must *first* be communicated with, worked through, and integrated within the personality *before* it can be disowned in meditation. Any suppressed psychic material gets channeled to the non-conscious areas of the mind from where it is projected onto otherwise neutral situations. This is a major cause of our neurotic symptoms and our interpersonal conflicts.

Also for those who have been socially or politically marginalized in our society or traumatized for various reasons, their inner voices have been squelched for too long. They need emotional support and permission to *first* find their voice by *permitting* their thoughts and feelings so that they can be heard, understood and their issues and problems finally resolved. Only then can disidentification be a useful method.

Also those with poorly formed ego 'structures' due to various developmental arrests, could bypass the need for processing 'unfinished business' in favor of the egoless state. This would amount to a regression to a pre-egoic state and get entirely confused with a genuinely transpersonal state of development.

Buddhism in the West is being challenged by women's greater participation and assumption of teaching and administrative roles within various Buddhist communities. Historically, this may be the most radical influence in the transplantation of Buddha's dharma in Western soil. The feminist perspective emphasizes interconnectedness, the importance of body, nature and intimate relationships. Its critique of Buddhism and religions in general, is that they have been historically male-centric, emphasizing autonomy, independence and achievement, while the more feminine qualities of connection, relationship and communion have been devalued. Such feminine qualities are a necessary counter-force to help balance the more prevalent androcentric qualities in all organizations, secular and spiritual.

Western culture has maintained the mind-body, male-female, culture-nature dissociation since its origins. The healing of this dissociation would emphasize *embodied* experience rather than detached observation, feeling to complement cognitive under-standing. Women place greater emphasis on embodiment and nature, healing and wholeness as opposed to the more male tendency towards emotional detachment, transcendence and spiritual attainment. Women's spirituality places greater emphasis on emotional bonding and communication, which could potentially heal the dissociation between men and women, and culture and nature.

Lastly, the feminist emphasis on embodiment and nature highlights the need to rediscover feminine faces for the sacred. This challenges Buddhist practitioners and communities to explore the interrelationship between our bodies and the body of Mother Nature. Discovering new forms of engagement and integration between ecology and the Buddhist sense of the sacred becomes of the utmost importance in rendering Buddhism's message relevant to the immediate global crisis facing our planet.

Within the ecological movement, we in the West are devel-oping wider, more inclusive images of personal identity that include indigenous and disenfranchised people from all over the world, as well as nonhuman life on our planet. We may be arriving at a novel understanding and expression of the Buddhist notion of egolessness or no-self, as we cultivate an ecological self, a more permeable sense of self that experiences our body as inseparable from the body of nature, the world, and eventually the cosmos.

II. The Path of Virtue

Chapter 1

The Power of Making a Vow

In taking the refuge vow we are held by the blessings of the Buddhist lineage. We can now afford to be vulnerable so that our experience feels as penetrating as an electric shock. When our heart is so open then one word of dharma can wake us up on the spot. But we have to be so ripe that as the seed falls, it sprouts at the same time. To have that kind of intimate contact with the dharma means that we're no longer wearing any armor.

The ability to stop the world and get off the mind's merry-go-round is the key to Buddhist meditation. In getting off the wheel there's a gap for a very brief period of time. In that gap there's no fear, no desire, no anxiety and no depression. It is the absence of all the samsaric or neurotic patterns and preoccupations. This refreshing pause doesn't last long. It's like a whiff of fragrance that quickly dissolves into air.

Through regular meditation practice we invite those gaps or moments of openness to appear with greater frequency and duration. If someone doesn't point out the meaning and value of the gap, it is not recognized because it is without distinguishing features. It may feel like a foggy, indistinct or blank state of mind. The usual reaction is to fill in this psychological space with subconscious gossip, problem solving, worrying or fantasizing.

The habit of thinking tangentially is so ingrained in us that it feels normal to be preoccupied with a variety of compelling concerns, but these are missed opportunities. This experience of gap appears in the spaces in and between our everyday activities. In the midst of an ordinary day when you find your attention suddenly drawn to the sound of the rain or the rustling of leaves, for a precious moment there's nothing but that sound.

Perhaps you notice the way light plays on the landscape as the sun is setting, illuminating shades of green, gold and auburn. For just that moment there is nothing but that rich perception. While showering you may momentarily feel the intense pleasure of warm water striking and stimulating your skin, or as you're shaving, there is just the sound *hssst* of your razorblade decapitating the hair follicles on your face.

In these instances the undiluted awareness of sight, sound and texture are complete experiences from which nothing is lacking. It may remind us of the same mindless joy we experienced as children, when we gave ourselves wholly to the taste of vanilla ice cream, or frolicked on the floor with our puppy or kitten.

As adults we have become so conditioned by our patterns of thought and behavior, and by our familiar social roles that our lives rarely sparkle with the spontaneous play of possibilities. The danger is that mindfulness could become a patterned ritual whereby we lull ourselves into a peaceful state, but are not really evolving on the path.

The great Buddhist teachers have suggested that our meditation practice should feel as if we're sitting on a razorblade. If we are cultivating awareness rather than comfort then our attention should have a crisp or sharp quality to it, a psychological edge that cuts through the tendency to nest. We no longer take refuge in anything that seduces us off the path of waking up, or in anything that does not support our path of sanity.

For this reason the idea of taking the *refuge vow* is very significant. In the Buddhist tradition we take refuge in the three jewels, in the Buddha as example, the dharma or teachings as the path, and the *sangha* or community of practitioners, as companionship.

When we take refuge in the Buddha we acknowledge that a human being with arms and legs, eyes, nose and mouth, who lived and died, actually woke up completely and totally. Shakyamuni Buddha is a stunning example to all of us that we have the potential to do the same. It is *humanly* possible to realize our true nature without divine intervention.

Our inspiration to take refuge in the Buddha is based on his *not* being a god, but as an example of someone who like us, was human and who struggled with confusion and desire, and yet succeeded in waking up spiritually. After six years of practicing the best spiritual methods that ancient India had to offer, prince Siddhartha decided to give up searching altogether. He sat down under the bodhi tree and didn't move until he completely unraveled his mind to its essence. Upon awakening to his ultimate nature, he was known thereafter as the Buddha, the awakened one.

The more subtle meaning of taking refuge in the Buddha is our growing understanding that taking refuge in the Buddha is simultaneously honoring our own inherent Buddha nature. Buddha awakened to a sacred dimension of *being* that is unconditioned, and radiant with an awareness that illuminates and outshines our human condition.

Taking refuge in the *dharma* means that we take refuge in the teachings as proclaimed by the Buddha and by the thousands of awakened teachers who have written commentaries on the original dharma. The Buddhist teachings offer a trustworthy map so we don't have to reinvent the wheel.

The deeper meaning of taking refuge in the dharma is that we relate to our life situation as the unfolding of the dharma itself. Our everyday life actually becomes the path. Whether we have fruitful employment and are wealthy, or have little money and are unemployed, whether we are married with a healthy family, or living a solitary existence, we do not have to leave our domestic situation and go to a more refined or exalted place in order to wake up. We take refuge in our life as a journey and work with what we have, rather than trying to transcend our circumstances.

Taking refuge in the sangha means that we are willing to walk the path and share our journey with our dharma brothers and sisters. Because of our commitment to meditation practice and to the teachings, we serve each other by embodying the teachings as best as we can. We share our confusion and our clarity, our neuroses and our sanity, and in so doing we dare to tell the truth to each other.

There is a loneliness that comes with the Buddhist non-theistic orientation towards life. It is the disillusionment that follows from understanding that we cannot depend upon a cosmic entity to save us. We're on our own, but we walk our path as lonely refugees *together* with our dharma brothers and sisters who keep company with us. Initially this loneliness feels like a problem, but then over time it sobers us up from wishful or magical thinking. Loneliness becomes the seed of compassion as we recognize that it is up to us to make life on earth abundant and meaningful.

Gradually as our practice matures the notion of sangha expands to include all people, all living beings, who share our planet. This larger version of sangha may be thought of as our commitment to stewardship of our earth.

Taking refuge marks the beginning of being an actual Buddhist practitioner in the formal sense. It's not compulsory, for one could continue studying and practicing mindfulness, and relating to other practitioners in a genuine way. However, there is a subtle meaning to taking the refuge vow.

Some of you may remember the time you initially met your current or previous partner. You happened to cross paths with this person and there was something about them that you liked. They caught your attention, provoking you to notice qualities about them that stuck in your mind. Little by little, this person got under your skin. When you weren't with them you thought about them. Perhaps on occasion you may have imagined what your life would be like without them, and a tear wet your cheek. At that moment you realized that you just crossed a line. That person mattered a great deal to you. This is a breakthrough experience which signals that your heart is open to another.

Thereafter you were able to 'see' or recognize what other people didn't see or recognize about this person. You saw them as beautiful, endearing, wonderful, intriguing. You found yourself open to them and 'tuned in' to the personal atmosphere that surrounded them. You had fallen in love!

It is only when we love that we touch and are touched by the other's essence, transforming this other into our beloved. In the same way, unless we fall in love with the dharma, it doesn't reveal its essence or secret. The dharma or Buddhist teachings need to keep company with us, but not as a super-ego that's judging us, but rather as a sense of brightness on the horizon of our lives.

When we fall in love with the dharma we are opening to the realization that our ordinary lives are personal expressions of the teachings. Whether we're happy or lonely, whether we're satisfied or dissatisfied, somehow we relate to our experiences as continuous reminders of the truth of impermanence, the truth of suffering and the truth of suffering's cessation. This is how we transform the ordinary stuff of life onto the path.

Falling in love with the dharma means that we are so open to the teachings that our everyday experience reveals subtle meanings and values. This heightens our perception and sparks renewed appreciation of our ordinary bread and butter world. We don't relate to our life as another tedious day or week to get through, nor do we become deliriously happy anticipating the weekend or a vacation as an escape from our everyday lives.

We begin to communicate with our claustrophobia, our aggression, our neurotic desire, not as a threat or a poison to discard, but as an accurate reflection of our immediate state of mind. Emotional upsurges and pervasive moods become personal resources that we're willing to acknowledge and refine. We don't have to throw anything away. That's what it means to fall in love. If our mate or our children have different styles of handling themselves or behaviors that are contrary to our own, we don't reject or divorce them because of such differences.

The refuge vow is a commitment to work with what life presents us. It is always important that we practice loving kindness towards ourselves, especially during challenging times. We make a commitment to stop beating ourselves up for being less than perfect. *Maitri* or loving kindness is a fierce discipline because it goes against our age-old habit of being our own worst enemy. It means that we begin making genuinely good friends with ourselves.

Extending loving kindness towards ourselves encourages us to be inquisitive about how we are, so that we can objectively witness the robotic quality of our lives, recognizing how patterned we are. With loving kindness we could look at those patterns with interest and critical awareness in an effort to discover creative ways of transforming them.

Becoming a refugee means that we're willing to be homeless and groundless in that we no longer take refuge in the very things that used to bolster up our false image of ourselves. This does not mean that we become emotionally distant from our husbands or wives, or disown our children, or give away our plasma TV to Goodwill. The idea is that we no longer take psychological refuge in the things that protect us from spiritual nakedness. We become much more vulnerable and this vulnerability is precisely what allows the teachings to penetrate us.

The transmission of lineage blessings enters our system so that potentially we could become a Buddha. Having taken refuge there's now a soft spot in our heart. Everything in our life becomes workable. We no longer see a separation between our everyday life and the dharma. There is a kind of sadness that is associated with this no-exit mentality for our constant companion, our internal echo or ego, has become less and less consoling. This absence doesn't have any resolution and does not get pacified by the company of others. Finally, we have given up all hope of escape. What remains is the immediate experience we're having at the moment!

Chapter 2

Even Real Men Need Loving Kindness

Extending loving kindness to ourselves creates a fierce fire. As we open to our shadow aspects, the broken, wounded and inferior parts, we may experience shame and feel diminished. Yet, it is precisely these forgotten aspects of ourselves that cry out for our love so that we can be healed and whole.

When various spiritual traditions and psychological schools offer descriptions of personal transformation, most of us wish to go from here to there, to go from where we presently are situated, to that place where we will be a transformed person. On the Buddhist path we are trained how to go from *here* to *here*, not from here to there.

Very often when we want to go from here to there, the mistake that we make is to avoid the parts of ourselves that are distasteful. In order to get *there*, to that new and improved 'me', we tend to deny or reject the parts of us of which we are ashamed: the part of us that feels like a failure, that feels defeated or broken, or perhaps the part of us that feels inferior. We're too quick to move away from where we are presently stuck or hurt.

The Buddhist path of mindfulness meditation begins by opening and allowing space to be exactly where we are. We can finally catch up with ourselves. The practice of mindfulness tunes us in to neutral psychological space so that we can reveal ourselves to ourselves. That is the essence of meditation practice altogether. You can light incense and candles, hang holy images in your room as part of the ritual, but personal transparency is the main point. We are allowing an opening without speeding towards the next thing to do, so that our body, mind and heart can unfurl and reveal themselves. If we are too ambitious, too goal oriented, we miss the broken, hurt, wounded parts of us, which need our solicitation and care.

Extending loving kindness to ourselves is absolutely essential. We are so ruthlessly hard on ourselves. I think that most of us would admit that we are highly judgmental of the inferior parts of ourselves; the very parts that we tend to deny or reject. However, every time we avoid, deny, or dissociate from the parts of 'me' that feel distasteful or threatening, we are abandoning ourselves.

It's as if we had a temperamental child whom we've neglected for a long time, preferring to give her a project with which to busy herself. The child is in a room at the far end of the house and is whimpering, crying out for attention, but we don't have time to be inconvenienced by her needs. We're so busy with the compelling stuff of everyday life that we don't want to break our stride.

At some point we actually have to walk up to the child, which is our own tender child-like self, open our arms and caress her, so that she could feel safe enough to find her own voice and speak her truth. Our stuck places, our depressions, anxieties and obsessions are symptoms of that unattended whimpering inner child. We tend not to listen deeply and sensitively to the parts of ourselves of which we are ashamed.

The practice of *maitri* is indispensable medicine on the Buddhist path. This is not a light and lovey kind of thing, but a fierce fire. Learning to love ourselves is the hardest work we may ever do. It seems contradictory to state that, but I think most of us know how true this is. It's very hard to love ourselves because of our ruthless self-judgments and our lack of forgiveness for being less than perfect. But there *is* a way to do this.

Randomly, at different times during the day, you might just pause for a minute and just allow space. This could be coordinated with a deep inhalation and exhalation, which doesn't have to be observable to anyone. You just get off the internal 'merry-go-round' and punctuate your immediate situation with a brief pause. Check in with yourself by bringing your attention to your heart or your belly. Tune in to your immediate situation with sensitivity and tenderness, as if asking, "How's it going?"

There's no need for analysis, or any kind of heavy-handed interpretation. Just an immediate 'hit' or reading guided by the question, "What am I feeling?" or "How am I, *really*?" We get a sense of whether we're feeling contracted and uptight, or coiled like a spring, whether we are feeling numb and empty, or experiencing a delightful fullness. To know that is wisdom. We don't have to fix anything. We begin maitri practice by extending loving kindness to the immediate feeling of pleasure or pain.

It seems obvious why our suffering would require loving kindness, but why would pleasure need maitri? Usually, when we experience pleasurable states of mind we want to hold onto them and prolong that good feeling. Or we want to 'stoke the fire' to enhance or amplify pleasure, or we get busy strategizing how to ensure that there will be a future supply. In subtle ways we are manipulating our experience of pleasure. Extending maitri is a gesture of acceptance and appreciation for the *immediate* experience of delight, openness and relaxation without any effort to make it other than it is.

In the practice of loving kindness, first we allow space in order to experience whatever is arising. Secondly, we cut the reflex to judge ourselves, and lastly we do not manipulate our experience by trying to *do* something with it. We allow it to be as it is.

Both our pain and our well-being have pregnant implications, if we are tuned in and 'listening'. We bring inquisitive attention or mindfulness to that feeling of well-being or discomfort until we feel we're ready to move on. There's no formula.

By allowing space we permit our feelings to speak to us. We might hear or recognize something different than our *belief* about that feeling. What starts off as well-being may change as we discover a pleasant facade camouflaging our underlying inertia or sadness. We might recognize that we're afraid to lean into a challenge. Instead, we have disguised a sharp edge into a dull pleasant space.

What we thought was boredom or claustrophobia may reveal our intolerance to relaxation or our hunger for stimulation. As we lean into the boredom itself, we may discover a peaceful sense of presence, an open buoyant quality that does not present a problem.

Many of us are constitutionally or genetically disposed towards anxiety. However, the *story* that we tell ourselves about anxiety or depression causes more pain than our genetic inheritance. That story grows over the years and decades.

We often experience more of the *threat* of anxiety, our catastrophic expectation about where anxiety is going to take us. "Am I going to fall off the earth or wind up in a psychiatric emergency room? Am I going to run out of the house naked, screaming at the top of my lungs?" Our personal story may be the larger part of our pain.

In my own experience with anxiety, when I'm confronted by a new emotional-psychological space that I haven't been before, it can feel like a frightening abyss. I've learned to ask myself, "What exactly is the territory that I'm afraid to step out into? What are my expectations if I go there?" When I name this place and observe this phenomena, the anxiety reaches a crescendo. Then I know what the hot button is. By dropping my personal narrative and by bringing attention to the *felt sense* of my bodily sensations and feelings, eventually the anxiety lessens in intensity and becomes tolerable.

Although it is madness, the easiest thing in the world is to shame and blame ourselves for being less than perfect, for not living up to our idealized image of ourselves. We might hear our mothers' or fathers' voices: "Look at you, look at you. How could you have..." or "There you go again". "Is that the best you can do? Why can't you be like your older brother!" When we start beating ourselves up, we're going backwards on the path of dharma. Negative judgment is very anti-maitri.

We operate according to a perverse logic. Somehow, we feel that if we extend loving kindness to the 'rotten' parts of us, they will get much more rotten. We think that if we love that part, that's like a secret wink, a handshake under the table, a hypocritical 'pass' on our weaknesses and personal deficiencies. Many of us feel that we should have gotten over it by now and do not deserve to be given any slack.

If we're going to truly transform ourselves we can't transform only the good stuff. We can't extend loving kindness only to our successful persona, the happy individual, the healthy functional person. We have to extend loving kindness to our *shadow*, the part of us that feels like a failure, that feels weak, insecure, that feels wounded. Loving kindness has to be delivered and extended especially to the parts of us that are suffering. This is very important.

There are gross and subtle domains of extending maitri. On an outer level, one of the ways that you practice maitri is to pay attention to your body and how you treat it. What kind of foods do you eat? Do you prepare nourishing meals or eat only what is convenient? Do you bother to sit down when you eat or do you eat standing up at the fridge while listening to the news? Do you take your time to actually taste what you're eating?

Do you pay attention to how you use your senses? Do you bother to appreciate the ordinary miracles of sight, sound, smell, taste, touch? Do you habitually listen to the news many times a day? Do you watch programs on TV that display graphic gratuitous violence? Are you permitting yourself to get toxified and drained by certain relationships that are no longer supportive of your path?

Whether you live in a room, a seven-room house or an

apartment, have you bothered to create a domestic space that feels good and uplifting to be in? Is your environment aesthetically pleasing? When you wake up in the morning does it feel good to wake up in your home? It can be one room with just a rug and one lamp, but if it's decorated with some sense of care and sensitivity then it could feel wonderful and inspiring.

The practice of maitri suggests that we pay *feeling-attention* to our life. We bring mindfulness to how we handle our body as well as the body of our world, the various environments in which we find ourselves. This represents the outer or gross expression of maitri. The more subtle practice of maitri encourages our feelings to communicate their message to us.

As a practicing psychotherapist there were many occasions when the living energy of emotions would dramatically reveal their wisdom when they were liberated from suppression or denial. One young woman in her early thirties entered my office in a state of depression and anxiety. She complained of many things, but stated that she didn't have a clue what the cause of her anguish was. After a series of questions I learned that she had an abortion three years ago when the man who impregnated her refused to assume paternal responsibility. Because of the emotional drama and turmoil around that painful event, she never grieved the loss of that unborn being, nor did she make amends for having to abort that being.

I suggested that when she felt ready that she could ritualize her grief and actually engage in a dialogue with the soul of that unborn child. Upon hearing these words, as if her denied grief got uncorked, tears began streaming down her face. Within several sessions her symptoms lifted. She had buried her feelings of grief and remorse and did not look back, but they took possession of her body and her mind, manifesting as anxiety and depression.

Learning to communicate with our own hurt feelings, with or without dialogue, is how we practice maitri. Paying attention to what we're feeling is not a luxury. That's actually how we walk the Buddhist path. Experiencing what is actually going on in our body, mind, and heart is meditation both on and off the cushion.

Lastly, a more profound way of practicing loving kindness, and this comes with a good deal of practice and personal development, is to make contact with the *sacred* dimension of life. Loving kindness in this context means we give *that* to ourselves. Through ongoing practice we have developed enough confidence to feel *worthy* of connecting with the hidden side of the natural world. We open our heart to the miracle of our existence which shines through the sights and sounds, tastes and textures of our everyday life.

As our mindfulness practice matures the invisible side of the phenomenal world discloses itself to our senses so that we can appreciate the miraculous in everyday affairs. This is not philosophy. In the immediacy of a naked moment, when we are fully present, the miracle of being is also present. This is the highest form of love you can give yourself. The practice of maitri is how we begin the Buddhist path, but also how we relate to the continual unfolding of our very life.

Chapter 3

Even Meditators Get the Blues

In the Buddhist tradition anger and lust, like other difficult emotions, contain wisdom if you know how to hold their energy and not get swept away. The energy of such emotions suggests a direction when we're not manipulating them. If you feel that you don't deserve to be experiencing such emotions or that they are nuisances to be discarded, then you can't utilize their wisdom aspect. The most challenging part of working with difficult emotions may be the recognition that they actually have something meaningful to say to you.

I think that here in the West we have a naive idea that meditation practice is supposed to occur in an airtight environment without fragrances, noise or movement. When someone starts coughing or sneezing in the meditation hall, some meditators judge this as a disturbance, and may wonder why this individual doesn't leave and take their annoying symptoms elsewhere. If someone enters the meditation hall late and needs to get settled, or if a cell phone accidentally goes off, or if another opens up her Velcro vest and it makes that unmistakable sound, these all create further disturbances and could provoke irritation and negative judgment.

One of the features of our personality that continually challenges our meditation practice is emotional reactivity. Based on strong emotions and hot passions, people go to war, get married and have babies, commit unspeakable atrocities, or create the artistic magnificence of the renaissance. We are driven by emotions to create both heaven and hell.

Many of us are fearful that we're going to lose our credentials as peace-loving Buddhist meditators because intense emotions threaten our hard-won equanimity. There's the amusing story of someone returning home after a meditation retreat, feeling very serene after sitting peacefully in a sacred environment. As soon as this happy yogi gets home his spouse or roommate reminds him, that before he left for his retreat, he forgot to pay the phone bill or that he left food in his room that is now rotting. He becomes instantly indignant and highly irritated as his meditative equanimity is sorely challenged. From tranquility we can go to resentment, rage and blame in a moment.

When we identify ourselves as spiritual practitioners we may feel that we should resist giving in to negative emotions like grief or sadness, anger and lust. Fearing that we're going to be overtaken or lose our composure and dignity, we set up a protective fence between ourselves and the upsurge of energy from our emotions.

Although it is understandable to create a barrier to protect ourselves from getting hurt, it becomes a problem because we have set up a conflictual situation between 'me' and 'my emotions'. There's 'me' and there's 'someone' who just pissed me off, triggering a wave of the negative emotion arising within ourselves. We're already on guard, fearful that we're going to be thrown off balance, and so we *react* to the emotion rather than allow it to communicate with us.

We tend to suppress the upsurge of such feelings and then fester throughout the remainder of the day. Alternatively, we could dramatize that intense feeling which is cathartic, but it doesn't help clarify our emotional pattern, because it fails to deal with the essence of the pattern. 'Acting out' is a reaction and as such, a distortion, because we are activating old conditioning which may have little to do with the present interaction. Either suppressing or dramatizing our emotions leads to further complications.

As Buddhist practitioners we should regard emotions as both a challenge and an opportunity. There's no such thing as a good or bad challenge. There's only challenge, but how we handle the challenge makes all the difference in the world. We usually regard life as either heaven or hell. When things are going well and the many parts of our life are working out smoothly, life feels like a blessing. At the drop of a hat, that condition can change radically. Something goes wrong with our health, our spouse becomes bored with us and no longer wants to be intimate, or our business begins to slacken, or a good friend insults us for reasons we do not understand. At such times, life feels like hell.

From the perspective of a meditator, these are challenges and opportunities on the path. The essential question is how do we actually roll up our sleeves and work skillfully with the energy of gnarly emotions on the Buddhist path? There are several methods each of which is very powerful. One will work better for some people, while others will find the alternative method more suitable.

The first method suggests that if someone has made us angry or upset, or for that matter, desirous or lustful, we immediately 'let go' of the person who triggered the anger or desire. Whenever negative emotion has been provoked by another we take that energy into ourselves and let that individual be freed from such distressful feelings. We hold the anger, or lust, resentment or frustration *within* ourselves, and we extend a heartfelt wish that, not only the immediate provocateur, but all human beings may be freed from such painful feelings.

According to Buddhist psychology it is most effective to let the person who elicited anger or desire 'off the hook' and use mindfulness to return our attention to the energy of the feeling. We boycott our story, our personal narrative, which gives us reinforcement for being angry, irritated, jealous or desirous. "Well, if he would've done that...." Or "She seems to be interested, or else why would she have....". Spinning a self-justifying narrative, could keep us stuck in a particularly stressful feeling for a very long time.

Using this method we free that person from being the 'culprit' and allow the feelings of anger, irritation or lust to be ours. We direct our full attention to the hurt spot by feeling into our body. We are mindful of any resistance we may have, as if putting up a wall to prevent the feeling from overwhelming us. At such times we ask ourselves, "What am I defending myself from?" "Who am I defending?"

Little by little we open, allowing ourselves to feel the aggression or the desire, and inquire into its nature. After letting the person off the hook, he or she is going to pop up again in our mind and this will trigger our narrative all over again, which fires up our emotions. We use mindfulness practice to cut the image of that person and again come back to experience the energy of our body-based feelings.

The basic point is that we bring our attention to the visceral gutsy feelings and stay with that for a minute or so. When we let someone 'off the hook', we let go of the *object* of our anger, jealousy, vengeance or lust. If that energy is not attached to someone or something, it begins to evaporate because it needs a hook to hang onto.

Another method of working with difficult emotions is to inquire into our pain through the vehicle of *dialogue*. This invites the feeling to come closer to us. We bring mindfulness and awareness to our experience of the these feelings. When we're feeling hurt by someone or something, or impacted in an overwhelming way, we ask ourselves what needs our attention or compassion.

Feelings are very complex and often don't lend themselves to immediate understanding. A good deal of our past interactions with others were only partially understood, and so we have a whole backlog of psychic material or psychic debris that's never been fully processed. Someone may look at us the wrong way or perhaps fail to give us the kind of attention that we yearn for, and suddenly the cork flies out of our emotional Champagne bottle.

In that vivid moment, asking ourselves what we need is a very powerful way to get under the emotion and discover what's really going on with us. When we feel something stirring in our guts, we could ask ourselves silently, "What is needing tenderness, love, or forgiveness?" We then wait for the wisdom of the emotion to reply.

When we discover a vulnerable sore spot we hold that space with tenderness rather than judge it or make up an action plan to eliminate the strong feeling. The first thing to do is to ask ourselves what needs *attention*, and secondly to ask what needs our care or *love*. We need to practice *maitri* or self-love, which permits us to hold a painful feeling without beating ourselves up or making ourselves feel wrong because we're hurting.

Meditation practice is a way of strengthening our ability to focus and direct our mind and our heart in a beneficial way. Ironically, extending self-love towards ourselves is very difficult. For many of us we would rather climb mountains, fight a thousand enemies before we would love ourselves uncondi- tionally. For us males it is even harder to love ourselves because it taps into the tender, nurturing aspect of ourselves, which is associated with the feminine, and this has been culturally taboo.

This practice of dialogue encourages us to communicate with the personal demons of emotional reactivity and problematic mind-body states. In meditation it is fairly easy to cut through thoughts by bringing our attention to our breath or to our body, but reactive emotions are very compelling. Once they have their teeth and claws in us, we feel swept away with anger or desire, sadness or fear. It is very hard to work with such powerful emotions using the mindfulness method alone.

Asking the painful emotion what it wants, or asking yourself what needs tenderness, love or forgiveness, connects us with the *essence* of that painful feeling. We are not nourishing or reinforcing the negative emotion, but instead we are communi- cating with our soft spot or vulnerability to understand what it has to say to us.

When we imagine our feeling responding to our question, we're tapping our intuition, thinking with our deep mind to get a sense of what we need to be OK. Once we learn how to dialogue with these distressful emotional states they begin to loosen their grip on us. We can still feel their energy but they take their fangs and claws out of our soft flesh. The painful feelings begin to get loose and amorphous as their fires begin to cool.

Rather than regarding the eruption of painful emotion as an alien experience from which we need to protect ourselves, we try to *befriend* our 'demons' by inquiring why it's hanging around in our body-mind. By dialoguing with the painful emotion, we *humanize* what we ordinarily reject as alien.

If we're feeling an upsurge of anger at ourselves for how poorly we handled a particular situation we inquire, "What about this whole thing is asking for attention and acceptance?" We may discover that we allowed another individual to make us feel frightened or anxious. We take this one step deeper by asking what exactly can't we accept about this situation? We may discover that we cannot forgive ourselves for being less than perfect, for feeling frightened or weak, confused or overwhelmed. We may have allowed an 'unacceptable' situation to happen and we didn't handle it skillfully, and this is the very thing that is asking for acceptance. The agitation and anxiety about our imperfection is the 'demon'.

It's important to allow meditative awareness to drop deeper and deeper until we actually touch that hot button and recognize what is under our skin that makes us feel so terrible. We then feed that with awareness, acceptance, and finally love.

We may be internally struggling with ourselves to not ever be angry, or to not be sad, or negative or depressed. We may be beating ourselves up for actually feeling powerless or confused, or because we believe that we are stingy or ruthlessly ambitious.

The more that we deny these very feelings, the more powerful they become, and the more distorted their eventual expression.

Everyday situations are the fertile ground for eliciting these negative feelings. Without the upsets, conflicts and disturbances of everyday life we would have no way to evolve our spiritual path. The ups and downs of daily life are the fertile ground for eliciting our unconscious patterns of thought, feeling and behavior.

We're continually being thrown of balance if we try to preserve an exclusively positive spiritual image of ourselves and maintain a life of peace and harmony. We do not want our neatly patterned existence to be abruptly interrupted because it sends our spiritual identity into a freefall. The strategic effort to defend ourselves from the rawness and unpredictability of life is the invitation to make peace and reconcile ourselves with the shadow side of life.

Chapter 4

The Broken Heart of the Bodhisattva

Those rare individuals who dare to approach the world with a tender open heart, who tirelessly meet human suffering with compassion, making their very lives a gift of service, are also the most self-actualized human beings.

The guiding vision and spirit of Mahayana Buddhism is embodied by the *bodhisattva*, the practitioner who has the courage to forsake his or her own enlightenment in order to work tirelessly for the benefit of all sentient beings. This is a huge commitment and an enormous vision. Although many of us are inspired by the vision of the bodhisattva, we may be taking a step forward with an inspiring vision, but our heart and belly are not integrated with our head. In our efforts to transform ourselves we are often led by our ideas and images but may not be going forward in our entirety.

We can't evolve spiritually unless all of our dimensions and aspects are cultivated. If our meditation practice is limited to the witnessing function, then we may be using meditation as a spiritual bypass, ignoring the body of our unresolved issues. We can misuse meditation as a way to skirt thorny issues to avoid listening to our hurts by labeling such pain "thinking" and then resume the ritual of emotionally distant witnessing. We do become less stressed and more relaxed, which is good, but we could be avoiding communication with our heart and belly, which often involves relating with our unfinished, unresolved karmic baggage. Meditation in daily life could be understood as a form of deep listening. It begins by making time to listen to ourselves. Through the ordinary process of living we have accumulated many hurts from the past that need to be digested and their lessons used as nourishment.

Many of us carry a good deal of unprocessed pain which needs to be sorted out. In order to heal ourselves from the various hurts that lie under our surface, it is necessary to first acknowledge that we are carrying something extra which hasn't been digested. We might ask ourselves whether there are people that we need to forgive. Are there individuals who we have excommunicated from our heart because they've hurt us in some way? These individuals may be our parents, our present or former spouses, our colleagues or friends, any one of whom may have failed to mirror us, or may have rejected, shamed or ignored us, intentionally or inadvertently.

We ourselves may have done things that were unskillful which hurt others, including those closest to us. We may have caused our children to resent and ridicule us because of things we said in a fit of anger. Way led onto way and we never apologized or made amends for our behavior. We may have made unwise decisions based on impulse that are still having repercussions to this day and we may still be blaming ourselves. Under the radar of our everyday awareness, we are hurting because of our own lack of forgiveness.

We have been both the recipients of hurt but also the perpetrators of hurt. When we get hurt by an interaction with someone, we tend to push them out of our hearts. Many men in particular often make the pretense that such conflictual and distressing occasions are no big deal, as if demonstrating that they can take it. But the body doesn't lie. This is what undermines our bodhisattva practice. We carry this pain within us. It lodges itself in the holding patterns of our bodily tissues and musculature.

If we feel that we have been unjustly attacked, disrespected or ignored, then a wall with barbed wire and electricity goes up. Not only do we exile this other person from our heart, but we block ourselves from feeling altogether. We cauterize or numb significant parts of ourselves so that we don't feel the pain. In so doing, we feel safer because the other person can't hurt us now, but by virtue of our wall of defense we also prevent love and tenderness from getting through to us. When we are on good terms with others, it is relatively easy to be generous and patient. When life circumstances are benevolent, we can afford to be grateful and appreciative. The challenge of the bodhisattva path is whether or not we can be generous and compassionate with others in difficult circumstances, and be appreciative of our lives when things are not going so well.

To prepare ourselves for the Mahayana journey of the bodhisattva, it is helpful to realize that any feelings of regret and resentment, or shame and blame, are opportunities for under-standing and forgiveness. One of the things forgiveness is *not*, is a 'pass' to the offending party. In other words, if we feel hurt by interactions with others, and we're able to forgive them through dialogue, it does not mean that we give them a green light to continue behaving in the same insensitive or offensive manner.

To forgive others means that we understand that at the time that they offended us they were behaving at a limited level of awareness where such behavior made sense to them. In other words, we see clearly that they behaved in such a manner because they did not see any alternative behaviors to the ones that they enacted. Compassion arises from empathy for our shared human condition. We do not need to punish them for their limited and confused reactions.

Forgiveness is not a one-shot deal but rather a process. We must first recognize that we are feeling hurt because of an inter-action with another. We tell the truth to ourselves. Secondly, we allow ourselves to experience the feelings of anger and sadness, blame or complaint, and regret or resentment. We need to recognize that we are feeling wounded and may be holding a clenched fist of defensiveness and animosity in our heart.

Bringing meditative sensitivity into this area permits us to *feel* what it's like to be vulnerable, or to hold a grudge and not want to give an inch. We might inquire of ourselves, "What does it feel like in my heart and in my belly to experience such resentment?" Rabbi Zalman Schachter said that when we hold onto anger and resentment by refusing to forgive somebody who needs to be forgiven, it's like taking a knife and stabbing ourselves in the belly in order to hurt that person who is standing behind us.

Erecting a wall of psychological defense to protect ourselves from further pain, siphons a huge amount of our life force to support these walls of defense. It also makes us insensitive and numb. The first step in the process of forgiveness is to recognize that we're holding onto something with a clenched fist. Secondly, mindful awareness recognizes that we are continually drumming up resentment, blame, and anger, to remind ourselves what a jerk this other person is, as a means of justifying our hefty defense budget.

Remaining defended reinforces our egoic identity and so we have an investment in remaining uptight. However the consequence of such defense is that we find ourselves feeling petty, stupid, or childish for not being able to let go of our grudge. At the same time, we feel that the offending party deserves to be punished by emotionally isolating them. Consequently, our body armor obscures the radiation of light from our inherent Buddha nature.

We don't realize that we are secret jailers. When we exile another individual from our heart, we've jailed ourselves. We now have to keep that individual in a cold dark place, and keep watch over that person so that he or she does not get close to our heart. The same phenomenon applies to exiling ourselves from our own love and care.

The key to forgiveness is recognizing how much pain that person was in when he or she caused us to feel anguish or distress. Again we use our meditative insight to realize that they were not in a place of clarity and compassion when they said or did that hurtful thing. At the moment that they committed what now feels unforgivable, they were a great distance from their Buddha nature. We contemplate the psychological distance between that person's neurotic behavior and their soul, or their inherent wakefulness.

When we are able and willing to *empathize* with how that must have felt to that person, to be at such a distance from their Buddha nature, the wall of our defense begins to melt. Our capacity for forgiveness grows as we understand how we also say and do things that are out of alignment with our own awakened nature as well. We glimpse the common humanity between ourselves and those who have hurt us.

Forgiveness doesn't always mean reconciliation and the restoration of a friendship. Sometimes we do not restore a friendship but we stop hating that individual. We make a commitment to ourselves, in our heart, to bring an olive branch to this relationship. We stop killing them in our minds with negative judgments and resist the temptation to repeatedly spin the same angry narrative. We refrain from reinforcing the walls of separation, and prevent ourselves from exiling them from our common humanity. This is a huge evolutionary step on the spiritual path.

A more subtle level of 'working through' on the bodhisattva path is the recognition that we may need to forgive *ourselves* for imagined failures. We may be holding a silent grudge against ourselves for being unsuccessful, for being unmarried and childless, for not marrying the 'right' person or having problematic children, or for not being beautiful, thin or wealthy, or for not aging gracefully. Perhaps we refuse to forgive ourselves for 'missing the boat' in life, for not being where we thought we should be on the grand chessboard of our life.

We could meditate faithfully for years, but in our heart of hearts we know that we're disappointed with ourselves. We have not gone beyond the *madness* of silent shaming and blaming of ourselves. This signals that we need to have a deep dialogue between these many dimensions of ourselves, or we will not be able to walk the bodhisattva path.

Often we feel emotionally assaulted or undermined not by a person, but by a life circumstance or situation. One definition of samsara is, wanting who or what you can't get, getting who or what you don't want, or getting who or what you thought you wanted only to discover that you're still dissatisfied. Many painful things happen that don't appear to have a guilty party to blame. We may have to forgive god or the universe for allowing our loved ones to die prematurely and abandon us forever, or for our life circumstances being terribly problematic, or for our genetic inheritance not providing us with the innate capacities to get to the top of the mountain of our life.

Such disappointments and resentments make us very heavy and hold us back. The bodhisattva path requires that we do not take samsara personally. There is a Zen saying that even if the sun were to rise from the West, it doesn't break the bodhisattva's stride. We walk our walk uninterrupted by the seemingly whimsical and capricious quality of life. We cultivate the commitment that life as it is, is sufficient for our journey of compassion. We still regard all situations as occasions of auspicious coincidence, containing pregnant possibilities that beckon our exploration.

The practice of forgiveness furthers our path by allowing us to begin mending our fractured heart. As we eventually learn to forgive even that which is unforgivable, our heart opens and permits a renewed flow of energy so that we feel alive once again in the place where we were numb and shut down.

There's a nonrational part of forgiveness that transcends ego's logic. Such forgiveness is when we choose good in spite of evil, the right thing in spite of the seduction of doing the easy thing. As embryonic bodhisattvas we make a dignified gesture in spite of the wrong that was committed to us. We know rationally that this person 'deserves' to be criticized or retaliated against, but we choose goodness over and against our impulse to retaliate, either physically or emotionally. This is what makes the bodhisattva's virtue of generosity transcendental.

This is our challenge if we are going to walk the path of the big vehicle of the Mahayana, where the fastest ways to cut through our suffering and that of others, is to make our life a gift or an offering. We use our life force, our intelligence, our virtue, our money, our time, or whatever else is available in order to be of benefit to others. We practice the benevolence of the bodhisattva, forgiving even that which seems to be unforgivable, so that we can unconditionally offer ourselves to others. This is the spirit of the Mahayana aspect of the Buddhist path.

Chapter 5

The Warrior Spirit of the Mahayana

"Let us not think that because we are less brutal, less violent, less inhuman than our opponents we will carry the day. Brutality, violence and inhumanity have an immense prestige that schoolbooks hide from children, that grown men do not admit, but that everybody bows before. For the opposite virtues to have as much prestige, they must be actively and constantly put into practice. Anyone who is merely incapable of being as brutal, as violent and as inhuman as someone else but who does not practice the opposite virtues, is inferior to that person in both inner strength and prestige, and he will not hold out in such a confrontation."[1]
Simone Weil 1

The Buddhist tradition states that in addition to sitting meditation practice, the gesture of making a commitment or vow is essential in furthering our dharmic journey. For most of us our mind is very fickle and there's so much in our lives that is seductive, fascinating and distracting. The habitual patterns that comprise our personality are very resistant to change, and our inferior side or shadow camouflages itself from our awareness, dividing us against ourselves.

Making a vow cuts through the hunger to continue shopping for experiential possibilities to relieve our boredom. At a particular stage of the path when we feel inspired to further commit ourselves to the practice of the Buddhist teachings, we take one of several vows.

Many people may wonder why this gesture is even necessary if we are serious practitioners. Perhaps this is similar to the difference between living with a lover as opposed to getting married. Exchanging vows with our beloved before friends and family becomes a public proclamation. Having invited extended family and friends to such a formal occasion makes it very difficult to say to your partner the morning after, that you think you made a mistake.

The ritual of taking a vow sanctifies and empowers a new state of consciousness and a new identity. Such a ritual prevents self-deception, as the meaning of our marriage vow continues to reverberate. The marriage vow marks our commitment to not shy away from what is difficult or painful, but to stay present and to share the journey with each other. Something has shifted as our personal boundaries now include a significant other.

Buddhism is a developmental path divided into three major sections. At the Hinayana stage of the path, practitioners who want to commit themselves more deeply to the path take the *refuge vow*. We take refuge in the three jewels: in the Buddha as the example or model of enlightenment, in the dharma as the body or map of the teachings, and in the sangha as the community with whom we walk the path. These are our fellow Buddhist practitioners with whom we form a bond of trust and camaraderie. We commit ourselves to telling the truth and allow ourselves to be transparent before such trusted friends. This becomes a paradigm for all future relationships.

In taking refuge in the three jewels we become refugees. We forsake the false refuge of believing that something outside of ourselves could actually rescue us and provide lasting safety, security, comfort and certainty. Taking the refuge vow is an expression of groundlessness but also freedom in that we no longer rely on an external savior. This is the meaning of the Buddhist non-theistic perspective. We assume full responsibility for all those little resistances inside of us, all those places that are in conflict. The fruition of the Hinayana stage is that we liberate ourselves from ourselves.

At some point in our practice we begin to discover some kind of soft spot, some place inside of us which we can't defend from the world's pain. This place feels somewhat wounded, as the suffering of others really penetrates us. As we mature spiritually, we allow the world to make a claim upon us.

Our growing sensitivity that other beings are suffering, that animals are suffering, that Mother Nature is suffering because of human exploitation, not only penetrates us, but inspires us to be of service in some way. This is the seed of genuine compassion and the beginning of the Mahayana or big vehicle.

This is not to say that practitioners at the Hinayana level do not feel the pain of others' suffering or do not feel compassionate. It's a matter of emphasis. The second major stage of the Buddhist developmental path, the Mahayana, emphasizes selfless compassion predominately. Simultaneous with the birth of compassion is the recognition that our skin-encapsulated ego does not entirely enclose us and separate us from the world.

At the Mahayana level we realize that we are animated by something that is much larger than our ego. That something is formless and profound. It is called 'bodhicitta' in Sanskrit, which means awakened heart. Bodhicitta is the active aspect of Buddha nature that motivates us to roll up our sleeves and step out into the world to make a difference. At that point in our spiritual journey we take the bodhisattva vow, as we aspire to forsake our own enlightenment until all beings wake up to their inherent sanity and basic worth.

A word of caution is warranted. We could become a total nuisance to everybody by acting as a professional do-gooder and trying to help out when we're not wanted, or trying to help others when we haven't sufficiently prepared ourselves. It is very necessary that we work through our personal issues so that by the time we are willing to work with others, we're very processed. In taking the bodhisattva vow, we make a commitment not to add any further pollution to the world. This means that we take full responsibility for our projections, for how we dress up the world according to our beliefs, assumptions and expectations.

We make a public proclamation before our teacher or spiritual friend that we're willing to have total 'skin in the game' of life and be of service to others. Traditionally, it is said that we're now willing to be a bridge, a highway, or a ferryboat to carry others across the ocean of samsara. We're willing to actually be used by others in order to promote their welfare and their progress on the path of waking up. Shouldering the burden of the world in order to promote the best in others is the bodhisattva's slogan.

This may sound like either the biggest ego trip or like religious masochism. It could be, if our gesture or commitment is based on ideology alone. The key is that we have had a change of heart, a complete shift in attitude. Having discovered our own awakened heart through meditation practice, we feel inspired to work with others without a goal orientation or self-congratulations. We aspire to be of service knowing that we are not finished products ourselves.

The paradox is that in our constant effort to put ourselves last and others first, we make enormous progress on our spiritual path because it is no longer self-centered. Every gesture of generosity transcends of ego's logic and allows the formless wisdom of Buddha nature to move through us.

Once we embark on the bodhisattva path we need a discipline to go about doing the work of compassion. There are six transcendental virtues or *'paramitas'* in Sanskrit, that are guidelines for how to fully manifest compassion. The bodhisattva path begins with the practice of generosity or *dana paramita* which is the heart of all the transcendental virtues. Such generosity transcends the usual dualistic categories of greater and lesser, generous and stingy.

Transcendental generosity means that we're willing to use our irritation, discomfort, and self-defensiveness, as steppingstones in working with others. There are numerous daily instances in which situations and people test our patience to the max without even intending to do so. You may be having a computer glitch and so you call tech support, where there is a time-based fee. You've waited twenty minutes to get a live person who then transfers you to another representative. After speaking with three individuals, the third representative asks you to please hold on for just a moment. You're really at your edge, and then abruptly you get disconnected.

In another instance you're waiting in line to buy a ticket for a concert, and the person in front of you purchases the last ticket. Your Friday night is now punctured with more empty space than you know what to do with. On another occasion you're on your way to meet friends for dinner and after searching for a parking spot for 15 minutes, you finally spot one. You pull your car up to parallel park, but before you are able to pull in, someone with one of those little minis, zooms in and takes your spot.

In each of these scenarios we tend to get triggered and experience either the instinctual fight or flight reflex, or the paralyzing default position of 'deer in the headlights'. The virtue of generosity challenges us right there. At that very moment we are reminded of our bodhisattva vow. We practice working with our own irritation, anger, and negative judgments of others for the *sake of others*. We save them from being targeted by the energy of our own negative feelings.

This does not mean that we sidestep a necessary conversation when having to deal with conflict. Having owned our own agitation and negative judgments, we're more able to speak to the heart of the matter without blame and without having to be 'right' while making the other wrong. What makes our gesture transcendental is that we're not trying to behave according to a spiritualized image of ourselves or according to Buddhist ideology.

Each of us is going to have to cut through some aspect of our own fear and hesitation in order to discover how we solidify situations usually because of our past conditioning. It's useful to pay attention to the associations that arise as we try to express generosity in everyday situations.

In one interchange with another there may be the memory of our mother scolding us and making us feel shameful. In another situation, we may get images of our father speaking to us in a demeaning manner, making us feel small. When these things happen, although they are demoralizing and painful, they are also gold. We get to understand what causes our defensiveness. That's how we start working with generosity.

When others mistreat us, the Buddhist tradition recommends that we regard such offending individuals as precious teachers because they help us practice equanimity in the face of adversity. This must go hand in hand with *prajna*, the eyes of the transcendental virtues. Prajna is that aspect of mind that cuts through our *idea* of ourselves and the world. It is crisp and crystal-clear perception free of our personal story. Because prajna is a double-edged sword, it swings back to cut our conceptualized version of ourselves, so that we don't take credit for our acts of generosity.

Our expression of generosity must be an outgrowth of developing prajna, or else we will not have the clarity or emotional stability to handle such challenges. There are numerous instances when we've not been mistreated by others, but instead are intimidated or feel diminished by circumstances. We're beset by self-doubt and hesitation as we consider stepping into situations to make a positive difference.

The bodhisattva practice is to quietly take on the very pain of doubt and hesitation so that others will be free of such distress. Internally, we take possession not only of our own doubt and hesitation, but we imagine taking on the doubt and hesitation from which all people suffer. This does not add more distress upon us. We gladly embrace what demoralizes others, energetically liberating the interpersonal field from emotional pollution.

This completely reverses ego's logic and helps to free us in turn. We have already experienced that deep source of warmth, bodhicitta, the place within us that is animated with love and compassion, so that we are able to genuinely open to others without becoming defensive.

There are many levels of expressing generosity. We could make donations to our favorite charities. In particular, we might support the three jewels, the Buddha, the dharma, and the sangha by donating to the building of temples or the growth of meditation practice centers. When walking in the downtown area of our town or city, we might stop what we're doing in order to allow a homeless person to speak with us. We take a few minutes and we truly listen to this forlorn person, who desperately wants to be listened to. We allow him the space so that he can find his voice.

On another occasion, a friend in need calls us at 11:30 pm when we've already retired for the evening. It is very inconvenient because we have had a long day and now we're quite tired. We're reminded of our vow of generosity and we actually go the extra mile, allowing ourselves to be inconvenienced for the sake of another. At the same time, we're mindful that we do have to go to work the following day.

In another situation, we're having a tiff with our husband or wife or our neighbor, and everyone is pointing their finger saying that the problem is not their fault. No one is giving an inch. All parties involved are stuck in a big knot about who is going to take the blame and communication has come to a grinding halt. As an embryonic bodhisattva we might say, "OK, I'll take responsibility for this. It may be my fault." Suddenly that knot unravels, and the whole situation thaws out.

Does that mean that we should always be sacrificial lambs? No, it does not. Sometimes, when it feels right, we actually do take it on the chin just to lubricate a stuck situation so that there is a flow of communication again. This is not to be confused with masochism. It is an expression of *upaya*, in Sanskrit, skillful or creative communication.

Transcendental generosity goes deeper. It means that we give up private space, that we stop hiding from ourselves and from others. We're willing to come out from behind our persona or social face and share the truth about ourselves. The virtue of generosity means that we stop having private corners in our own mind. This is very subtle. All of us have little private agreements that we've made with ourselves. It's like a handshake under the table where one part of our mind keeps a secret from another part. We have all kinds of covert ways that we indulge in hypocrisy and self-deception.

On the bodhisattva path we renounce these private corners in stages. Becoming transparent to ourselves is the biggest source of generosity. As we become authentic human beings we are able to energetically transmit that level of ruthless honesty to others and liberate them from their need to hide.

Often transcendental generosity means that we help others to help themselves. We teach others how to fish instead of giving them a fish each and every day. Practicing generosity requires a great deal of skill and creativity. One expression might be to pacify or soothe a person who's very agitated, anxious, and uptight so that the individual is not jumping out of his or her skin. Or it may be a situation that embodies such prickly qualities that needs our tender and creative care. Being a bodhisattva is knowing what to offer to bring down the energy of such situations.

In another case, we may meet someone who is very insecure, suffering from low self-esteem, someone who has lost faith in herself. In this case, we might attempt to enrich or cultivate that individual so that she feels she has a foundation, an emotional safety net. By providing an atmosphere of safety and nurturance, she may feel confident to find her voice and her sense of grounding.

There are people who are holding back because they're afraid of criticism and censure, or perhaps are not in the habit of making their qualities visible to others. An aspiring bodhisattva may try to magnetize such individuals, drawing them out in a very creative way by eliciting their strengths so that they can feel adequately supported to show up.

We may encounter someone who is riding high on his self-importance and is making an aggressive display of arrogance. An advanced form of generosity is to cut through his trip by allowing space to outshine his display. A bodhisattva can shift his or her attention at will and not offer any reinforcement to such a person, who is now left with the empty echo of his inflated bravado. At the same time, we could manifest our genuineness and speak what is true for us, without attacking or trying to undermine this person. Our genuineness provides a stunning contrast to the other person's inflation.

The most subtle version of transcendental giving is not having any idea of 'me' as a 'giver', no idea of a gift, and no idea of a recipient of my gift. In other words, we do not take credit for our expression of generosity. What makes our gestures of generosity transcendental is that we don't make personal territory out of our good deeds by not conceptualizing ourselves as benevolent spiritual beings.

This morning it was very cold and a little foggy. I have a bed of flowers in my little garden. The petals of all the flowers were curled up into buds. As the sun rose and the temperature increased, the flower buds began to open in response to the sun. We could say that the sun had no intention to have that effect on the flowers, and that the flowers had no intention to open towards the sun. It just spontaneously occurred. Transcendental generosity is just like that.

III. The Path of Transformation

Chapter 1

Shining a Light in the Darkness

*"...If you bring forth what is within you, what you bring forth will save you. If you do not bring forth what is within you, what you do not bring forth will destroy you."*2
Jesus 2

There is a dark side of the mind that many meditators unwittingly avoid. We could meditate for many years and still be plagued by agonizing emotional patterns, dysfunctional behaviors, and addictions of all stripes and colors. Meditation usually does not shine a light into these areas because our 'shadows' are heavily defended. Mindfulness practice illuminates the parts of the mind that we are willing to see, but other parts operate mechanically beneath our radar.

Mindfulness practice reveals the transparency of the ego, who we take ourselves to be, but that is only half the story. We also struggle to *not* be the person who we secretly suspect we are. The *shadow* is the self that we have suppressed and this needs to be made visible. In other words, through meditation we could eventually see the transparency of our persona, the face of ego, while our shadow remains invisible as a psychological force that shapes our thought and behavior.

The *shadow* holds the wounded and broken parts of ourselves, the failed ideals, the fateful consequences of poor choices. It is the inferior, unprocessed, undeveloped aspects of our personality which we hide behind the social mask that we present to the world. These contradictory aspects of personality where we feel most vulnerable, weak, shamed and deficient are the very areas that we're most resistant to communicate with, yet they contain missing pieces of our wholeness.

The good news is that here in the West we have a golden opportunity to use two very powerful technologies. We have the Asian tradition of Buddha dharma, the teachings of the Buddha with its practice of meditation, and we have various schools of Western psychology, with their emphasis on dialogue in the helping relationship, with its focus on problem-solving.

Each map shines a light into the dark area of the other tradition. Buddhism shines a light into Westerns psychology's bias towards pathology and its conspicuous absence of soul or spirit. The Western psychological map shines a light into Buddhism's more universal approach, honoring individuality and illuminating the complexity of personality, while empha-sizing the importance of dialoguing through our problems and conflicts.

Each tradition defines the ego-self or personality differently. Psychology emphasizes its central importance, while Buddhism rejects its existence as anything more than a seductive illusion. Yet, both must still grapple with the problem of self-identity. Let's look at the process of personality formation from a cross-disciplinary perspective.

Every infant learns to become a very sophisticated actor or actress and learns in order to gain membership into its family. As much as an infant needs oxygen, it needs parental love and affection, and it will do whatever it takes to secure these emotional supplies. In the process it takes on the qualities and characteristics of the family and culture within which it finds itself imbedded.

Every infant develops a 'survival kit', an adaptation strategy to insure its physical and emotional survival within its family. This emergency plan is adapted to defend its very life, and so is created under some degree of duress. Thereafter, every child will automatically resort to this bundle of patterns without commu-nicating with the whole being that it is. This bundle of patterns *is* the ego-self or personality. The human dilemma is that this adaptation strategy interferes with the natural wisdom of the whole being that we are.

Every child is socially conditioned to identify with its personality. As we mature, we identify with the part of us that reflects how we like to think of ourselves. "I'm a successful accountant, a dynamite sales rep, a crackerjack computer programmer, a nurturing mother, a devoted father, an inspired poet, a competitive jogger". Ironically, the aspect of ourselves that needs the most loving-kindness is the part of us that we don't want to look at. This is called the shadow aspect of personality, a term of phrase coined by the Swiss psychologist CG Jung.

The rejected or disowned shadow self is a natural consequence of the ego building process, consisting of those qualities that were forbidden or denied by the family of origin. The problem is that the rejected, unacceptable and unacknowledged qualities accumulate to form an inferior personality with its own thoughts, feelings and behaviors. These split off unacceptable portions of ourselves to form a shadow or alternate personality. The shadow does not want to be revealed or known and so it feels alien to us, like a dark twin or evil other.

The shadow may be the part of ourselves that didn't achieve what we set out to achieve, or the part that feels broken and wounded. It is the inferior personality that lives invisibly behind our persona or social face. Like looking at the sun, trying to observe our shadow directly has a blinding effect. We don't see our shadow objectively but instead encounter it in other people who trigger our own denied and disowned qualities.

When we deny or block parts of ourselves, it is a psychological law that we will *project* those very same qualities onto others who seem to have a 'hook' upon which to hang our disowned qualities. The stereotypical examples are gay bashing by men who vehemently deny their own homosexual tendencies, or religious wars which become the bloodiest of battles, because each group feels that god is on their side, and that their enemy is the embodiment of everything evil. In these examples we virulently project outwardly our internal fear and self-hatred.

The problem of the shadow is not its real psychological existence, but its denial. In our effort to eliminate the pain of recognition of our own dark self, we refuse to own our possible greed, hypocrisy, cowardice, our obsessions and addictions, and our capacity for destructiveness. In seeking to avoid contamination with such imperfection we tend to manufacture 'enemies' who become sacrificial scapegoats, imagined embodiments of what we have disowned in ourselves.

One way to begin shining a light on our own darkness is to reflect on our family of origin. Every family, like every organization, has a blind spot that it prohibits from being seen. In the family it becomes a black psychic hole. Every child growing up in a family gets either a verbal or nonverbal message not to go there. This is the place that we are likely to deny as well.

Children tend to fall into this psychological hole and unwittingly carry the family shadow into another generation. For instance, just like our parents, we may feel uncomfortable hugging and touching others. Or perhaps we feel embarrassed to speak about toilet functions or sexuality, or about money or death, or we are loath to express sadness and grief. At the same time, based on our family conditioning, we may justify our explosions of anger, which feel empowering to us, as they force others to come out from hiding behind their façade.

In a family with a depressed mother or father, cheerfulness and humor are encouraged as a camouflage against the underlying atmosphere of unhappiness. The unspoken message to the children is, "Don't bring your long faces to the dinner table because they're too threatening to this family". Another family may emphasize the qualities of strength and toughness, handling your life with swagger and bravado. This becomes a camouflage for avoiding feelings of tenderness, vulnerability or weakness. The message becomes, "Stop whining. You're acting like a baby?

If you have to cry, go to your room and shut the door".

In another family one of the parents is positioned as the all-knowing authority, who expects submission by the other family members. The family message is, "Your mother or father knows what's best, so don't bother thinking on your own". The unspoken message to the children is not to think or act independently. This becomes a camouflage for avoiding the parents' fear of their children's budding individuality as well as the threat that their authority will be challenged.

In these examples, the parents' underlying message prohibits certain feelings, attitudes or behaviors, thereby conditioning their children to inherit the family shadow. The shadow quality in our family of origin is emotionally charged because of our parents' guarded attitude around it. Sometimes it manifests as an attitude of avoidance, squeamishness or defensiveness.

The shadow is like a silent underground stream that runs beneath a city. It is a silent 'other' that runs underneath our persona, but which becomes accentuated when we love or hate, or experience intense jealousy or anger, or when we feel utterly buoyant and celebratory. It often breaks through the cracks in our self-image or persona when we are experiencing extreme emotion.

If we're going to transform ourselves as meditators, and walk the path of the Buddha, we need to make a relationship with our shadow. This involves looking directly at our familial inheritance and our own denial system. On the surface, this is obviously contradictory, because it means that we are shining the light of awareness onto what we would prefer to keep dark.

The way that we recognize the shadow is by its vehemence, the intensity of our emotions that are disproportionate to the faults of the targeted individual or group. While shopping at the mall we might witness several teenagers with sagging trousers and carrying skateboards, who are laughing uproariously. They seem to us to be oblivious to the other shoppers and lack all sense of propriety. We immediately become judgmental and angry.

Perhaps *we* are oblivious that our own rigid control over the urge to let loose and be silly has just gotten triggered. The stark contrast between our own 'goodness' or 'rightness' and the teens' 'wrongness' is the tip-off that we are in shadow land.

This kind of black and white thinking and blind negativity can be found in racism, male chauvinism, class warfare, homophobia and gay bashing, which are examples of collective shadow projection. As meditators, when we are working with our shadows, we are dealing with something that has immense implications.

When we find ourselves becoming completely upset with another over an inconsequential interaction, it is at *that* moment we might recognize our reaction as disproportionate. This becomes quite apparent when we realize that any ordinary individual would not be having the same reaction as ourselves. One method is to look directly at the triggering situation and inquire what exactly is provoking our emotional reaction. Why are we getting so agitated?

Another method to elicit your own shadow is to engage in a self-dialogue, asking to speak to different parts of yourself. This can be done with a partner or you can do this through journal writing. For instance, you may ask to speak to the part of yourself that is shamelessly uninhibited, or the part of yourself that is unambitious and lazy, or ruthless and opportunistic, or perhaps the part of yourself that is fearful, needy and dependent. You call forth one of your hidden faces and engage it in a dialogue, as a way of looking behind your persona.

A third method to smoke out our shadow is to describe in detail an imaginary or actual adversary or enemy. Without editing your initial feelings, describe how dislikeable, disgusting, immoral, or horrible this person is. This imagined individual probably contains qualities that are completely opposite from your own, qualities that you have forbidden yourself from experiencing, and consequently which have been buried. Welcome to your evil twin!

A word of caution. It is important not to psychologize an actual experience of victimization where you were either abused, exploited or violated by another. If there were traumatic incidents that continue to provoke intense feelings of disempowerment, grief, fear or rage, these qualities probably do not reflect your personal shadow. Such feelings may be part of a collective or *existential* shadow which includes disease, death, war and other catastrophic events that life delivers to us for no apparent reason.

The question naturally arises, "Does that mean that we all are just like our enemies, horrible, disgusting and immoral?" No, but because we have rejected certain taboo aspects of ourselves, they have become distorted, magnified and emotionally charged over time, and now appear to be either grotesque or exceedingly shameful. They do not represent our totality, but are psychological islands that have split off from the mainland of our wholeness.

Whenever we shine the light of mindfulness and awareness on our unconscious patterns, we are disidentifying with them. Working with the shadow begins by first acknowledging its existence, recognizing that it is emotionally hot to touch, and understanding that it is highly resistant to conscious recognition. We then shine the light of awareness into what we have denied and disowned, our own darkness.

We are taking ownership of what we have discarded and projected onto others. As we bring together our missing parts we become more complex beings. Our vices, our imperfections, our neuroses and our dark passions, reveal something essential about our human nature, something that needs to be worked through and not abandoned. *The shadow holds our buried potentials.*

The shadow includes the unlived life because we can't be fully alive if we are crushed by secret fears and shame. As we learn to make a relationship with the shadow dimensions of ourselves, our identity expands immeasurably. We are reclaiming psychological territory which was formally 'held' in an unconscious domain. This results in feeling less need to block, deny, suppress, or dissociate from emotionally painful experience. Working with our shadow can heal us by increasing our capacity to be alive, to be whole and therefore to be more present to our surrounding world.

On the Buddhist path we extend maitri or loving kindness to our shadows so that we are more able to make a relationship with the entirety of ourselves. We practice loving the broken parts, the vulnerable and wounded parts of our personality. To our surprise, we might discover that the shadow contains tremendous energy which could be used to further our dharma path.

Through the process of disidentifying from who we think we are (persona) and from who we are afraid of becoming (shadow), we come closer to embracing our true identity as the profound formless depth at our core. That is, when we hold our shadow in tension with our persona, identifying with neither, we are closer to experiencing our egoless Buddha nature.

The Buddha proclaimed 2600 years ago that the self we thought we were, did not exist. Perhaps in the 21st century, integrating meditation with shadow work will bring us closer to this realization.

Chapter 2

Befriending our Demons

The usual reaction to our thorny emotions is to regard them as if they were demons. We either retreat from them, manipulate them to minimize their impact or we fight with them in the hope of conquering them. Such reactions are based on a lack of confidence and ultimately do not work. Buddhism suggests that we allow such problematic feelings to just be there. We stay grounded in our body and remain open to their suggestions, befriending our demons rather than keeping them as enemies.

There's a tendency to make the sitting practice of meditation an oasis, something separate and different from ordinary life. It feels good to cultivate silence and stillness and leave behind everything that is troubling, confusing or overwhelming in our everyday world. We could develop a bias that when we sit in meditation we should be above and beyond the fray of ordinary life, but this creates a radical contrast between ordinary life and our meditative process, converting meditation into a method of escape.

The Buddhist practice of mindfulness meditation discourages this kind of dualistic attitude. Instead, it encourages us to stay anchored in our body, present with whatever is arising for us. Many schools of Buddhism encourage meditating with our eyes slightly open in order to take in light. This grounds us in the recognition that there is a real sensory environment that surrounds us or that we are sharing silence and stillness together with a group of people.

Over time our mindfulness sensitivity should pervade the activities of ordinary life so that eating breakfast, taking a shower, combing our hair, or spilling milk and then having to mop it up, all become opportunities for practice. If we truly want to transform ourselves we have to make peace with our persistent problems, issues and conflicts, or our demons. Buddhism encourages us to appreciate our demons because they prevent our meditation practice from becoming overly dreamy or transcendental. Demons bring us down to the ground of where we actually live.

Demons could be our unprocessed feelings of grief, sadness, guilt, the pain of loneliness, the fear of intimacy, the threat of a meaningless existence, the ongoing anger and frustration with various people, the age-old resentments that life did not bring us what we wanted. These unprocessed or unfinished issues complicate our lives and bring us great suffering.

It is quite difficult to bring about any real fundamental change in ourselves when we have interior places from which we ourselves are hiding. We can have insight into why we shouldn't smoke cigarettes or marijuana, or why we shouldn't overeat or oversex, and even be able to articulate the details of our compulsive patterns to our therapist or our meditation instructor. Yet, when those urgent or desperate feelings arise, most of us don't tolerate the emotional pain very well. Often we don't even recognize our patterns when they arise, but instead find ourselves swept away by their compelling power.

It is common to deflect our awareness from those painful places and fill ourselves with our habitually distracting activity. Pain is often regarded as an obstacle to our meditation and not as the very path of meditation itself. This is a universal problem. Most meditators pride themselves on not indulging in blame, complaint, regret or resentment. What may not be obvious is that many practitioners tend to deny or suppress such 'non Buddhist' feelings. Once we disconnect from such distasteful feelings, we develop defenses to block our awareness from recognizing them.

If we avoid experiencing a visceral 'felt sense' of our feelings, unwilling to drop down into their raw nitty-gritty quality, we tend to develop body armor to defend ourselves from experiencing such rawness. The body might become an embodiment of psychosomatic symptoms in the form of depression or anxiety, headaches, food disorders, or various allergic reactions that have no medical basis.

Befriending our demons permits us a rare opportunity. We get to see how we unconsciously magnetize painful situations to ourselves in order to unpack experiences that have not been processed properly. By intentionally communicating with our demons we connect with what urgently needs our attention. Dialogue with our demons brings back these split off or discarded aspects, so that we may become whole. Interestingly, the word 'heal' comes from an old English root 'haelan' which means to make whole.

One of the ways to discover our demons is to relate with our body as a source of wisdom. In the practice of mindfulness of body, we bring our awareness to our sensations and the sensory world of sight and sound. We may be able to 'hear' the language of the body more easily than the language of the mind because it is simple, concrete and straightforward. Usually we experience the threatening or frustrating aspect of negative emotions, and don't trust where painful feelings are going to take us. We think that there's no profit in fully experiencing our painful feelings, so we shift our attention from our body to our head, and relate with them in a defensive manner.

When powerful emotions threaten to overwhelm us we tend to either suppress or dramatize them, but rarely do we allow their full expression. That takes the sturdiness and confidence of spiritual warriorship, a willingness to open ourselves, trusting in the energy of the emotion. Buddhism encourages a no-nonsense approach in working with the irritations, upsets and frustrations of our ordinary life and the vivid upsurge of our reactive emotions.

There is a method in Tibetan Buddhism called, 'feeding the

demons' popularized by Buddhist teacher, Tsultrim Allione. This practice encourages us to establish a relationship with our unresolved feelings, the very thing most of us are trying to get away from. Whereas our *shadow* is largely unconscious, demons are emotional knots or problematic states of mind which we are aware of, but which we are reluctant to actually feel. Because we have failed to honor our demons they demand our attention.

Feeding our demons is a psycho spiritual process. We dare to make contact with the very thing that's causing us to suffer, instead of pushing it away. We let it come into us and we actually communicate with it, attempting to understand what it is hungry for. One demon may want our tears because we have been holding onto grief over our mother's death, and so the demon causes depression and inertia to remind us that we need to weep. In another case, our demon wants us to open up our heart and speak with someone who we have exiled from our life. This demon may cause our body to feel rigid, uptight and numb. Perhaps our demon is there as a migraine headache urging us to leave a relationship that died on the vine five years ago.

The task is actually to work with your demon in stages. First, we acknowledge what the issue is. Secondly, we take notice whether this conflict or issue has something to say to us. Thirdly, we actually open ourselves up and listen with our *heart* in order to recognize that there's something valuable in this distasteful state of mind. When we feed the demon and befriend it, it stops being a demon. We no longer need painful reminders of unfinished business.

Voluntarily marching into emotional pain for ordinary people sounds like madness. It is completely counterintuitive because we think that we should get rid of our demons rather than give them nourishment. The meaning of the practice is that we're trying to integrate the parts of ourselves which we have denied and disowned. Feeding our demons is a creative way to make contact with these neglected parts and invite them into a meaningful relationship, so that *we* can move on.

The discipline is to cut your personal narrative and bring your full awareness to the energetic aspect of the emotion, which is felt most directly and immediately in the body. One way to begin to work with the practice of befriending your demons is to inquire whether you feel cheerful or uplifted in this present moment. Usually there are a number of problems and conflicts that have gotten under our skin and are bugging us on any particular day. After asking yourself this question, let everything come up that is immediately concerning. Don't try to list every single problem you can think of, but only what is particularly stressful to you at this moment. It is important to keep a little distant or detached from them so that you don't trigger an enactment of the whole issue and set off a cascade of negativity. This is a method adapted from *focusing* created by Dr. Eugene Gendlin.

The next step is to choose the one problem or conflict that is most problematic. Bring your awareness to your body in order to experience the sensations and feelings around this particular demon even if it is not perfectly clear. Try to get a sense of what the *whole* thorny issue feels like.

If you're having extraneous thoughts, use the mindfulness technique to cut through tangential thinking so that you can bring your attention back to the issue at hand. You're trying to get a 'felt sense' of the most distressful demon, what it feels like in your body, rather than merely observing it.

Ask yourself what the outstanding quality of this particular demon is. Try to come up with an image or word that really captures what it is. Is it anger or depression, a feeling of sadness or claustrophobia about a relationship or possibly a feeling of being lost, as if you've missed the boat in life?

When you accurately identify your demon, the recognition itself often causes a subtle shift in your body. Again, use the mindfulness method to cut through any tangential thoughts and come back to the raw sensation in your body. Ask yourself whether there's a good fit between the word or image and the living quality of your demon. If there isn't, then try again to come up with a word or image that accurately captures the essence of the demon.

Sometimes what is most distressful in our life is not one thing, but the way in which many things have congealed causing us to feel trapped. Sometimes it may feel like our whole life feels stuck. In that case, the word 'stuck' or 'trapped' or 'overwhelmed' or an image of being bound or in a small enclosure, might be the best term or image to capture our demon. If our life feels ambiguous and uncertain, perhaps the best statement to use is, "I don't know" or an image of walking through fog.

When you think that you have an accurate image or term for your demon, let yourself feel that for a minute or so. Don't interpret or narrate and don't try to figure out a solution for it. Let yourself be with that demon for a while to see if it communicates something to you, remembering to keep a safe distance. One of the ways to move this process along is to ask yourself what the worst thing is about this demon or emotional knot.

The next step is to inquire what it would take to appease this demon, for it to be at peace. Alternatively, you could ask yourself what it would take for *you* to be OK about this demon. Use the mindfulness method to cut through any fabricated answer that you come up with, and wait for something to spontaneously emerge.

What is essential is to be open to the demons' communication to you, that is, to honor the natural intelligence of your emotions at the level of raw energy. This is precisely how we feed our demons, and eventually befriend them. We respond to the demons' suggestions by acknowledging their communication. The suggestion may be that you leave your job, move from the city to the country, leave an old relationship, begin a weight-loss program, make amends with people whom you've hurt, practice expressing gratitude for your life, dare to start all over again, or make peace with what is irreconcilable. Such communication offers direction or guidance, but you do not have to make any radical changes at the moment based on this revelation.

We take an attitude of appreciation that our demons spoke to us. We have liberated them from imprisonment by allowing their energetic presence to be felt in our body. This is precisely what opens up our bodily contractions and defenses. We don't have to *become* a demon, but we do need to value what our demons have to say to us. They remind us that we have refused or forgotten to acknowledge or act on something that was crucial, and that's why we are suffering. Directly relating with the felt sense of our feelings seduces them to reveal what *we* have concealed from ourselves.

That's how we bring about personal transformation. We go to the place that is most distasteful, the part of us that we do not want to embrace, and we make friends. Yet, some demons return again and again, each time in a different guise, and we must repeat the process of asking what they want. The key is establishing a meaningful relationship with what we have refused to relate with. When we do this with the courage of a warrior, eventually we are able to *deputize* our demons, enlisting them as helpers on the path who remind us to use adverse circumstances to fuel our spiritual journey.

Chapter 3

Meditation as the Art of Everyday Life

We entered the world with a sense of the miraculous, with openness to raw experience, but by the time we leave childhood, we were taught to suppress the ordinary miracle of being. The problem is that the world is no longer enchanted for most of us. We no longer find ourselves in a world that pulsates with life, as when we were as children. The sense of the sacred in everyday life has mostly been lost. Yet, our youthful wish for the superlative does not vanish.

Buddhist teachers are frequently asked by their students how to practice mindfulness in everyday life with all of its distractions and demands, and how to make a connection between the inspiration and clarity that you feel while performing sitting meditation, and walking the path of ordinary life?

A Zen Buddhist teacher may abruptly exclaim, "The apple blossoms have arrived early" or "That blind man's tapping cane," drawing the student's attention to the everyday world *as* the path. Buddhism is a non-dual path where we relate to our everyday world as very much part of our meditative journey. Yet, our lives are distorted by the wish to be relieved of our boredom, our emptiness, our emotional flatness and from our silent worries.

Cultivating hopefulness, the promise of better things to come, seeking entertainment and distraction, hungering for dramatic experiences, all permit us to briefly escape from ourselves. We could define *samsara* as the misguided urge to find a remedy for our dissatisfaction, our boredom, and our sense of emptiness, in all the wrong places.

Mindfulness practice reveals how we are percolating with

constant restlessness, too impatient to fully look, hear or feel the events of our everyday life. Assuming that everything in our lives is more or less the same becomes an excuse for not needing to be inquisitive. In our hunger to find something that is distracting, exciting, hopeful or self-confirming, we tend to overlook the seemingly inconsequential details of our everyday lives, but such details *are* the path.

The secret of how to bring meditation into everyday life is to make room for boredom, for the ordinary. We have to trim our eagerness for the 'extraordinary' and cultivate a willingness to not titillate ourselves with our own internal channel surfing.

The practice of mindfulness as a way of life, involves paying meticulous attention to those momentary gaps in our discursive thoughts where we can experience silence and stillness. From these gaps we can momentarily perceive a naked world, free of our beliefs and assumptions, our hopes and fears, all of which distort the clarity of the world.

For our everyday lives to become an *art*, the practice of awareness is indispensable, in distinction to mindfulness. Buddhist meditation involves both mindfulness and awareness. Mindfulness or *shamatha* is the dispassionate observation of our mind's contents with accuracy and precision. Panoramic awareness or *vipashyana* is tuning into the larger space within which these contents arise.

Vipashyana is the inquisitive aspect of mind that lends meaning and value to the individual thoughts, images and feelings that arise in sitting practice. It is an expanded awareness and appreciation of the forms, textures and colors of our sensory world. We must cultivate an unlimited openness to hear, touch and feel both our inner world and the outer phenomenal world, permitting both to 'speak' to us in their own language.

Inquisitiveness never becomes stale, because we can never exhaust all there is to know or appreciate about ourselves or any other thing or being. When we relate to our world in a very personal and intimate way, we perceive a living, breathing world, a sacred world, not a world of inert objects and anonymous entities.

Usually when we perceive such an ordinary thing as a chair, table or our couch, we feel bored because such things are so ordinary, so familiar and uneventful. When we bother to pay attention to the details of our everyday world, we might walk into our home this evening and notice that we feel a special fondness for our soft leather recliner, which is remarkably comfortable and inviting. It has supported us for the past 15 years as we read books on Buddhism and online news from our laptop computer. This recliner has caressed our body like an affectionate mother, supporting us so that our mind could be free to entertain lofty ideas. As we feel appreciation for our recliner, it seems to come alive, to take on character.

There's a strong temptation to ignore what is beautiful or exquisite in favor of what is practical or profitable. Yet our human heart has a logic of its own which is often at variance with our habits. To live with awareness is to live at our depth. It is to live close to the heart where we are open to beauty, love and the sacred, as well as to feelings of emptiness, loss and despair. This depth offers us an expanded context or atmosphere for these experiences, adding richness, texture and tone, and expanded meaning.

Vipashyana or panoramic awareness, is like taking a different seat within our mind from which to regard our life situation, viewing the things and beings of our everyday world as intimate partners. Without appreciating the surrounding *openness* in which everyday things take their life, we don't perceive them in their innocent vitality, in their natural vividness.

The gong that I am presently using is a relatively new one. The one I had before lasted about 35 years, until I accidentally dropped it on my way to a mindfulness class! When it hit the ground it made a dull sounding thud and I knew it had come to a sudden death and would never resonate any longer. I was instantly heartbroken and this was not just a poetic sentiment.

I bought that gong at a Zen monastery store in Japan. That gong had been with me to many meditation retreats, and I had practiced with that gong at my side as my faithful companion for many years. For me, it was alive and had soul. When I struck it every morning it made that wonderful resonant vibration, as if to say "good morning", and my world was set right.

I could not throw the gong away or recycle it. Instead, I made a place for it on a shelf in my meditation room, where it is not forgotten. The point is that when we relate to our world as a living world, and not as one surrounded by lifeless objects, then we transform an otherwise material world into a living sacred world with soul.

When we look at the world through our heart it becomes an artful way to bring the meditative state of mind to our ordinary life. Life becomes a work of art when there's naked perception which sees the world as *it* is, not as we would like it to be. When we are present in this way, the world reveals its *presence* as well.

The world's presence is revealed through natural symbolism which doesn't need to be interpreted in order to be understood. It could be the bubbling sound coming from an urban water fountain which arrests our attention. Our whole sensory world might stop, and there is nothing but the enchanting sound of water playfully splashing on cement, as if it had a life of its own. Such intimate communication between us and the phenomenal world allows the world to reveal its soulfulness. Such symbolism or imagery is a reconfiguration of perspective in any sensory field, yielding a refreshing and novel way to see and feel the world.

After meditation practice this morning I went for a short hike. The wind blew a crisp yellow autumn leaf across the pavement, which made a scuttling sound. All I could hear in that moment was the lonely 'voice' of that autumn leaf which immediately consumed my attention. That leaf was the essence of autumn, of all the autumns that ever were or will be. It was a unique embodiment of the endpoint of the natural cycle of the four seasons, symbolizing both nature's fruition but also death.

I felt melancholy and had an intimation of my own death but not from a depressed point of view. Instead, my imagined death in that moment, felt like a part of the natural order of things, part of a lawful cycle that is timeless.

In order to heal the split between our inner world and the three-dimensional hard realities of ordinary life, we could be open to the suggestive or metaphoric aspects of life. Every aspect of our world needs love and attention so that it may reveal its hidden side. We could engage the events, situations and relationships of our everyday life within an expanded framework, the enlarged atmosphere of post-meditation awareness. We could be open to experiences, not for the sake of overcoming life's struggles, but to appreciate life fully.

Such an orientation towards our everyday life has immense energy and the potential to reframe the mundane incidences of our life with meaning and significance. It may also enable us to see patterns of connection that help us understand our human existence, our place in the immense design of things.

One of the primary functions of meditation practice is to cut through the tendency to make our world conform to our expectations. In order for naked perception to occur we must open to the neutral psychological space that is always already there. Out of a willingness to experience spaciousness, a brilliant color emerges and interrupts our train of thought, a sound shatters our discursive thinking, someone touches us gently and our hearts melt. When we perceive ordinary phenomena in this naked fashion there is an abrupt discontinuity in the usual flow of things. This is what allows us to see things in their innate essence and nature.

This is how we bring meditation and elegance into our lives.

We use all of our senses in order to be in total communication with the world, understanding that the world exists in sympathetic relationship with our five senses. There's some kind of underlying communication that's taking place all the time between our senses and the surrounding environment.

We suffer from the madness of not recognizing that we are embedded in relationships not only with our family, friends and colleagues, but also with the natural world and the ordinary things of everyday life. We tend to see separate events and isolated spheres of activity in the world. Such a view of life leaves us without a coherent image of ourselves or our world.

Buddhism teaches that both we and our world are *mandalas*, coherent and integrated systems of orderly-chaos where opposite, contradictory qualities mingle to form intricate combinations. The natural world is intelligible when we are not struggling with it, or trying to escape to a better place. The human mandala is a self-organizing, integrated system with ourselves in the center and our surrounding world as the circumference. This suggests that our world *belongs* to us, and we to it. Through this perspective we establish a sense of belonging and connection with our world.

The center of every mandala exists as open space with inconceivable depth and vastness. From ego's point of view, this basic space is boring, uneventful, deficient and desolate. But from the Buddhist perspective, unless we learn to appreciate this neutral psychological space, we cannot cultivate art in everyday life.

In this open dimension there is a complete absence of struggle, preoccupation, and the demand that experience will rescue us from ourselves, from the doubt that we may not exist as we imagine ourselves to be. When we are relieved of this preoccupation there is vast openness, as layer after layer of our projections and preoccupations fall away. We can't help then noticing that each moment and each thing is truly unique.

The way that we transform our ordinary life into a work of art is to appreciate the ordinary miracles of sight, sound, smell, taste and touch. Without our senses, the phenomenal world would be a flat two-dimensional affair. The five sense doors are middlemen that permit the phenomenal world to arise within our awareness, penetrating us, and making love to us through our body.

Panoramic awareness or vipashyana is the power to sense the formless background from which objects, sounds, fragrances and textures arise and to which they return. It is this realization that gives rise to the qualities of playfulness, spontaneity and creativity. In the crisp immediacy of nowness, we recognize the unrepeatability of each moment and can witness the uniqueness of everyday things.

Art in everyday life is the deepening or intensifying of experience that gives new significance to the ordinary things of our world. It is feeling the breath of life pulsating in and through the ordinary events and activities of our everyday world. We might regain a childlike sensitivity to the immediate freshness of *this* moment. Here we are unashamedly more fully alive, already enjoying an abundant life which can no longer be exhausted.

Chapter 4

The Alchemy of Personality: Buddhist Perspectives

A central doctrine of Buddhism is the notion of no-self or egolessness. This appears to emphasize the universal aspect of enlightenment while failing to honor the human person who has been walking the spiritual path. The teaching on the five buddha families and the six realms describe various styles of individual struggle in transforming neurosis to sanity. Here, we discover the human personality and its various expressions of madness and mindfulness.

The Western psychological tradition, although acknowledging an unconscious dimension to the mind, presumes that our identity lies with our personality or ego-self. The assumption is that the personality's web of relatively stable patterns is who we are. Western psychology views our human development as occurring within the boundaries of the personality and its relations, but with few exceptions, does not acknowledge an underlying spiritual essence.

From the Buddhist perspective, our personality patterns do not reflect *who* we are, but rather *what* we've become based on disconnection from our underlying essence or Buddha nature. Each personality type is a metaphor, a compensation for having dissociated from our essential nature and a distorted search to regain it. In other words, with meditative clarity, the structure of personality is seen as a distorted replica of our Buddha nature.

Interestingly, the Sanskrit root term for 'mindfulness' is *smriti*, which means, "to remember", "to recollect" or "presence of mind". This does not refer to remembering the past, but presence in the here and now. The implication is that when we are completely present, we remember our original nature. Forgetting who we truly are, we then identify with the various aspects of our personality, our personal narrative, our social roles and the habitual behavioral patterns, all of which make up the feeling of 'me'. This is how we 'fall' from grace.

As practitioners of meditation, we need to question whether we really are our personality or whether there is something more profound that is shining through our persona. If we carefully inspect our modus operandi, it seems as if our personality is trying to replicate our essential qualities but in a confused way.

For instance, we may work out religiously at the gym in an effort to become as shapely, physically impressive and powerful as we possibly can. We unavoidably have to stick with our strict regimen in order to feel that continual sense of vitality, strength and beauty. Consider the possibility that on some level we're trying to *imitate* or enact the spiritual quality of strength, power and beauty. Ironically, these primary qualities are actually part of *who* we are on a very deep level. Self-existing strength, power and beauty do not require continual reinforcement when we remember to tap into them as dimensions of our very being.

Perhaps we feel that we don't properly exist unless someone makes us the center of their world. Urgently needing to be loved and cherished, we continually find ourselves magnetizing others' attention in an effort to gain acceptance and affection. We may be mimicking the spiritual quality of love or lovability, trying to convince ourselves that we are worthy of being deeply appreciated. No amount of external feedback is sufficient to satisfy us until we embrace our innate lovability and loveliness. At that point we no longer pull for admiring attention.

We may work tirelessly to feel a sense of personal achievement and accomplishment, but no amount of achievement or success seems to touch our core. We may be mimicking the naturally existing virtue of fulfillment, which is, being in a state of completion, *already* being accomplished. When we are fully present with head, heart and belly, we're able to ride the currents of situations as they naturally unfold and feel complete, whole and satisfied without the compulsion to fixate on the goal of achievement.

Buddhism does not address personality explicitly but does describe basic styles of thought, feeling and behavior in the teachings on the *six realms* and the *five buddha families*. The 'five buddha families' are modeled after the five natural elements of earth, water, fire, air and space. We each tend to manifest the qualities of one element more than the others, although we each contain the qualities and characteristics of all five elements. The elements are neutral self-existing energies which can fuel our life journey towards enhanced sanity and health or deepening neurosis and imbalance. The choice is ours.

We could think of Buddha nature as clear light shining through a prism, refracting into five cardinal colors. Each color represents one of five basic styles of relating to our human situation, in either neurotic or exalted expressions. When we forget who we are at our depth, our essential Buddha nature, we experience an aching sense of deficiency, a feeling of personal lack.

We're all very eager to get rid of our neurotic patterns on our way towards becoming more refined human beings. But this approach is going backwards. Real transformation means that we must use the manure of neurosis to fertilize the flowers of mindfulness and awareness. In the more mature stages of Buddhist practice we reach into and *feel* the earthy energy of neurosis. The path of transformation involves working with our personality patterns at the level of elemental energy and going with their flow, unimpeded by discursive thought.

Each of the five archetypal qualities represent five ways for how we, as individuals, can work with our mind, our interpersonal strategies, and how we can transform our problematic emotional patterns. Buddhism teaches that we can transmute the neurotic aspect of this energy into its exalted form by taking it back to its source. It is important to keep in mind that we each have *all* five wisdom elements within us in different proportions, but we're more disposed toward one element over the other.

The Buddhist teaching on the *Six Realms* describe six fundamental styles of struggle based on forgetting our naturally awakened Buddha nature. Because of our disconnection from what is most real in us, we try to compensate for this enormous loss through distorted and ultimately frustrated searches for 'being'. From this perspective, samsara or the 'human condition' is based on our dissociation from our true nature and the futile search for symbolic substitutes for who we already are.

The term, 'realm', describes an entire psychological atmosphere or environment. Each of the six types of 'personalities' brings forth a particular realm due to a specific conflict and style of struggle. We do not simply perceive a world that is already given, but we co-create a world based on a cognitive distortion, a specific motivation, an emotional pattern and a behavioral strategy to remedy what we feel is missing. In other words, we tend to project our distorted inner world of overvalued thoughts and feelings onto the outer world which, in turn, shapes our inner world.

The Buddhist perspective is that our personality and the environment within which we find ourselves, are on a continuum, and are not separable. The realms are also transient and therefore open to change and transformation. We can potentially transcend the limitations of each realm and evolve to a less conflictual condition. Eventually we can reconnect with our original or essential nature and no longer spin through these realms on the wheel of samsara. Or we can devolve to realms of greater confusion and suffering based on the distortions of how we view ourselves and the world.

Each of the realms is associated with a specific wisdom energy, one of the five natural elements of either earth, water, fire, air or space. Each realm portrays a specific personality type with a particular motivation and challenged by a particular psychological *demon*. The term 'demon' refers to the cluster of problematic thoughts, attitudes, feelings and habitual behaviors that plague both our meditation and our lives.

Understanding the six realms and their relationship with the wisdom energies of the five Buddha families provides a useful map for how to transform our personality, as well as to help clarify our meditation practice. The individual within each realm experiences a personal deficiency or lack, and tries to remedy this sense of absence. Each realm involves preoccupation with a *secondary* struggle, while ignoring the primary problem, which is disconnection from our original or Buddha nature. Understanding these dynamics guides us in working creatively with our neuroses.

The realms do not have any specific order, so the sequence of this presentation is arbitrary. As human beings we can find ourselves situated in any one of the realms, based on a combination of our genetic or karmic inheritance, our early family and cultural conditioning, and the particular choices we are making in the present, all of which reflect our level of awareness. Each of the realms has a spectrum of possible expressions, ranging from neurotic to a pathological extreme.

According to the Buddhist iconographical painting of the *wheel of life*, the bodhisattva Avalokitshvara appears in a different guise in each realm to offer a creative method of liberation to the suffering individual stuck within the realm. The most significant aspect of the Buddhist perspective is that the six realms and the five Buddha families are considered fluid *transitional* states which we can positively transform with particular skillful methods, enabling each of us to exit from the binding unsatisfying aspects of our lives. Ultimately, we are able to do this by remembering or recollecting *who* we are at our depth.

The God Realm: Transforming the Self-Inflated Personality

The god realm is associated with the Buddha family of space, which is the awakened quality of radical openness and infinite possibility. It is our innate wholeness, the indescribable totality of ourselves which is profound, incomprehensible and without any fixed perspective.

When we confuse our true identity with our overvalued thoughts of ourselves, we disconnect from the wisdom energy of space and we try to imitate its qualities of profound peacefulness and imperturbability. We create a distorted lifestyle that is artificially buffered from conflict, criticism, vulnerability and ambiguity. Surrounding ourselves with 'yes' people who affirm how wonderful and accomplished we are, reinforces a grandiose sense of self-importance.

The *demons* of the god realm are ignorance, denial, dissociation and lack of inquisitiveness. We are intoxicated with ourselves, and live a carefree life dedicated to comfort and ease, but have forgotten the true purpose of our life. Although we do not suffer from gross pain, paradoxically, the very absence of suffering deprives us of the motivation to reach for what is most real and true.

The god realm mentality is not defined by the actual achievement of success, but refers more to a self-congratulatory state of mind. As a god realm personality we believe that we are superior or unusually unique, and expect others to recognize us as such. From this inflated self-appraisal we don't believe that we need to work on ourselves any longer, and if we encounter conflicts, they surely are the fault of others.

Our interpersonal relationships are typically strained because we are so preoccupied with our own glory that we've become insensitive to the needs and wishes of others. In order to maintain this bubble of self-proclaimed wonderfulness, we try to surround ourselves with people who reflect that condition back to us. We don't want to hear negative feedback or any kind of corrective criticism because that would deflate our intoxicated status. We protect our bubble of intoxication by skillfully reinterpreting critical feedback or disregarding the validity of others' perspectives, to justify our exalted status.

In traditional Buddhist iconography the god realm inhabitants are depicted as being made of light. They have used meditation as a form of absorption so that they can transcend the problems and conflicts of the human condition. They float above the earth in an imperturbable state of mind, defended against the existential condition of having to deal with conflict, struggle, ambiguity and confusion.

The *pathological extreme* of this realm is the Narcissistic personality. We inflate our self-importance as if to imitate the utter expansiveness of space, outshining everyone and everything else. We have exaggerated fantasies of unlimited success, power and ideal love as if we were kings and queens of the universe. We could actually be accomplished musicians, writers, chefs, nurturing parents, skillful therapists and creative teachers, or *imagine* ourselves to be so accomplished. Through highly selective attention we only see what positively mirrors our glorious self-image.

We may have co-opted spiritual and psychological methods as a spiritual bypass to avoid dealing with the nitty gritty problems of life. Consequently, the pain of this realm comes from eventual disillusionment. One day an abrupt shift occurs as events rupture our airtight cocoon.

We may find that our spouse or intimate partner has become bored with and critical of our chronic inflation and our self-congratulatory stories. Or perhaps an otherwise procedural routine medical checkup reveals a serious condition, requiring further testing and assessment. The business that we created which has provided us with a sense of great accomplishment, may now be in the red due to unexpected competition. Or perhaps we have lost our muse and no longer feel inspired to be creative. Our confident and reassuring smile has become rigid and forced.

Self-doubt infiltrates our bubble as we suspect that we may have *manufactured* heaven. Our inflated sense of being superior and our expectation of unlimited success and ideal love becomes suspect. With this doubt we fall to earth.

In the painting of the wheel of life, the bodhisattva Avalokiteshvara appears in the god realm playing a lute in order to rouse us with the sound of the dharma, which 'speaks' the truth of impermanence and human suffering. This potentially awakens us from self-complacency and inspires us to allow the truth to penetrate our armor. We might open ourselves to others' feedback and instead of rationalizing our failures and short-comings, we allow both positive and negative feedback to coexist. We could strive for a more realistic self-image that integrates *both* positive and negative self-images.

With the exception of the pathological extreme of Narcissistic Personality Disorder, the god realm personality can be trans-formed into a realization of the unique occasion of human birth and the preciousness of all human beings regardless of their lack of achievements. By exercising inquisitiveness, we might dare to see ourselves in our true stature without need of self-inflation.

In order to transform ourselves as god realm personalities we must permit ourselves to experience our feelings particularly when we don't feel reinforced by others. We don't allow ourselves to tune out of situations that are threatening to our inflated status. Eventually, we sustain our attention long enough to communicate with our inferior or shadow side in order to gradually integrate it within the personality. As we move towards greater authenticity, we may remember who we are at our depth.

The virtue of the god realm is the discovery of the wisdom of openness, the capacity to just be, and to confidently enjoy simplicity. In simplicity there is no need to maintain rigid boundaries separating our positive from our negative qualities, or ourselves from others, and so there is no need to inflate ourselves. Finally, we can allow ourselves to be as we are.

Old habits of personality die hard. The god realm personality may continue to have problematic relationships due to the lingering need for continual admiration combined with a disregard of others' needs. This lack of empathy could sabotage friendships and romantic relationships, and leave this personality without sources of positive mirroring. We may begin to wonder where did all those good years go, and with that thought find ourselves struggling to regain what was lost.

The Jealous God Realm: Transforming the Competitive Personality

This personality type is associated with the wisdom energy of wind, which is the breath of life, the rhythmic circulation of energy in the world. It is the awakened quality of activity, growth, transformation and achievement. The movement of wind allows us to ride the energy of synchronicity or meaningful coincidence, as our projects are brought to completion by moving with the intelligent flow of life's natural rhythms.

Each personality style is a metaphor, as we try to compensate for abandoning our own Buddha nature by *replicating* aspects of our awakened nature. As jealous gods we strategize how to get back to an idealized promised land through competition and the thrill of success, which convinces us that we're on our way to re-gaining 'paradise lost'. In its neurotic aspect, when we forget who we are at our depth, we experience our own wind energy as a feeling of groundlessness. This condition creates anxiety, fearful insecurity, a lack of confidence and the need to be vigilant. Suspecting that we may have lost our way, our purpose or perhaps the meaning of life all together, we react with the compulsive need for achievement or hyperactivity.

When we disconnect from the Buddha family of the wind element, we try to imitate its qualities in a distorted form. As jealous god personalities we have some memory of moving creatively with the intelligent flow of life's natural rhythms and effortlessly achieving our purpose. We may not remember exactly when we lost this glorious time of life. Perhaps it happened by degrees, or in some cases it could've happened because of dramatic circumstances that deprived us of our imagined good life.

We may have gotten seriously ill, or lost a great job. Perhaps the love of our life divorced us, or a very close friend may have betrayed us. We may find ourselves in midlife suddenly wondering where all the good years went. Or perhaps we have always felt that in order to thrive we must 'win' in life or at least not allow others to surpass us.

Any of these may be trigger points that dramatically shaped our perspective. We lost the confident expectation that our life would always be sunny side up. As jealous god personalities we feel that we have little value separate from our accomplishments, and therefore our identity depends on a continual sense of victory and success. The shadow of incompetence and insufficiency plagues us as we anticipate not being able to keep up with the challenges of our life.

Our identity depends on a continual sense of positive momentum, but there is a nagging fear that we are not going to accomplish our life goals. Consequently, we feel driven from within to move faster and work harder. Like being in quicksand, the faster we hurry the more we feel that we're sinking under the burden of life's necessities.

The *demons* for the jealous god realm in meditation and in life are restlessness and agitation, compulsive busyness and inner drivenness, feelings of incompetence and fear of failure. As jealous god personalities we pride ourselves on our skill and intelligence in getting who or what we want in life. We are eager to reclaim more and more psychological territory through achievement and success, and are not timid in using our intense energy to get what we want. The thrill of anticipated success and the fear of defeat provides the jealous god personality with the edge of excitement, the sense of being more alive than others.

We may find ourselves at a friendly social gathering of old friends whom we haven't seen in years. We find it difficult to relax and enjoy ourselves for there is an inner compulsion to advance towards a victory or seek advantage of some sort. We find that the momentum of our own ambition provokes us to challenge others' views, question their accomplishments, find weaknesses in their arguments in order to feel that we are ahead of the curve.

The *pathological extreme* of the jealous god mentality may be associated with the sociopathic personality. The spirit of competition degenerates into the need to win at all costs. In its most degraded expression, the jealous god personality violates others' rights, and uses deceit and manipulation for personal profit or pleasure. There could be a quality of vengeance in their desire to reclaim what they feel has been taken from them, and so they ruthlessly grab whoever or whatever they want. Such individuals lack remorse and tend to rationalize their antisocial behaviors.

Alternatively, the other pathological extreme of the jealous god realm personality is the *compulsive* aspect of the Obsessive Compulsive Disorder. Here we feel compelled to keep endlessly busy and preoccupied with either the achievement of goals or with the need to get closure on various projects which continue to stack up. We suffer from an inner drivenness that cannot be satisfied.

Jealous god personalities tend to view other human beings as competitors for shrinking resources and so hyper vigilance, obsessive-compulsive behaviors, workaholism, competition and control become camouflages for their insecurity.

In the painting of the wheel of life, Avalokiteshvara appears to the jealous gods with a flaming sword as the symbol of force and power since this is the only language they understand. Avalokiteshvara, wielding the flaming sword symbolizing awareness, teaches them to 'fight' for their inherent wisdom and not for secondary satisfactions.

The virtue of this realm is the wisdom of all accomplishing action. As a jealous god personality we recognize that there are rhythms and cycles to our life, each having its own integrity. Through meditation we begin to trust the natural rhythms of our life and go along with their intelligent flow. We learn to tune into the naturally existing rhythmic circulation of energy both within ourselves and in the world. Like two tuning forks that eventually synchronize their vibrations, the sympathetic relationship between us and the world invites auspicious coincidences. This is the virtue of all accomplishing action.

As we begin to practice meditation we can objectively witness our compulsive need to busy ourselves with multiple activities, endlessly organizing things, attempting to make things work ever more efficiently. This painfully reveals the neurotic quality of air as we substitute action for genuine feeling. We learn to gradually punctuate the speed of our incessant activities long enough to experience our feelings, which are often confused with our thoughts.

As we reconnect with our inherent worth as a human being we cut through our misguided need to obsessively validate our existence. We renounce the mentality of win/lose, gain/loss, success/failure and instead try to experience pleasure and enjoyment by passionately involving ourselves in activities that we love. We practice moving along with the rhythm of natural cycles and circulation of energy.

Such circulation can be experienced in sitting meditation. In quiet reflection the very same principle animates our cycle of breathing, the circulation of our blood, the intricate rhythmic process of digestion, assimilation and elimination, the generation and destruction of every cell in our body and brain.

If, as jealous god personalities, we do not give up the symbolic struggle (through competition and achievement) to reclaim the psychological territory that we imagine we have lost, we could exhaust ourselves. In such a depleted state we may opt for a minimal one-dimensional life style.

The Animal Realm: Transforming the Habitual Personality

Both the animal and god realm personalities are associated with the element of space, the qualities of non-conceptual openness, unfathomable depth, innocence and simplicity. These qualities of space reflect our natural capacity to 'be'. For the animal realm personality, the experience of openness and possibility provokes a feeling of bewilderment. Spaciousness triggers feelings of desolation, inertia and depression. As animal realm personalities, we react to space by going deaf, dumb and blind in an effort to hide from ourselves.

When we dissociate from the wisdom energy of space we try to replicate its qualities, but in a distorted form. Spaciousness becomes 'spacing out' or the freezing of space. The animal realm offers the comfort of diminished awareness and sensitivity, mimicking the imperturbability of space.

The cognitive distortion of the space element is to feel that we have no distinguishing features, that there's nothing about us that really stands out that would attract anyone's attention. We tend to feel unimportant and unworthy and so we blend into social situations. Believing that we are not intrinsically worthy, we boycott our own wishes and instead seek emotional homeostasis to minimize any disturbance to our imperturbable space-like quality.

The animal realm mentality is characterized by instinct, a very habitual way of doing things. We take comfort in the limited boundaries of habit, but this creates a dull, monotone and minimalist approach to life. Although we enjoy the mindless comfort of hibernating we are apathetic concerning self-understanding and inner growth.

We might find a comfortable niche in the post office, or working in a bookstore, or on an assembly line, or taking tolls on a bridge, or in any job that involves the performance of rote chores and procedures.

We feel compulsively driven to behave in habitual ways not for pleasure, but to relieve the stress of change and uncertainty. We could be excessively devoted to work or domestic chores and projects, but not make time for leisure activities, relaxation or friendships. In friendships and romantic relationships, we tolerate only a limited repertoire of behaviors and range of feelings, and have unreasonable resistance to spontaneous play, tenderness and humor.

Animal realm mentality slavishly adheres to daily rituals, typified by having the same things for breakfast, eating the same foods at the family deli, Chinese or Italian restaurant. Although there may be no less than 28 things on the menu, we will order spaghetti and meatballs as we have done for as long as we can remember. We find it repugnant to arouse inquisitiveness because this would involve exploring new psychological territory and the possible threat of change. Such feelings disturb the emotional evenness of the space element.

The *demons* in meditation and in life for this personality are lack of inquisitiveness, inertia and laziness. There is a neurotic fear of being overwhelmed by too much to figure out as life's problems feel too complex to understand or control.

Alternately, our life may feel dull and uninviting. The predictability of our jobs, our marriage, our money problems, our familiar relational conflicts all feel like an emotional plateau with no promise of uplift. The only way to handle it seems to be to 'check out', to dissociate from our immediate situation. When confronted by an inability to control or understand something, we feel incapable or stupid. Any psychologically or emotionally charged situation could trigger the paralyzing fear that we will drown in an ocean of murky feelings.

The *pathological extreme* for the animal realm may be associated with both depressive disorders and addictions. We just want to basically numb ourselves so that we don't have to think or feel. We are unwilling to arouse inquisitiveness because of fear of what inquisitiveness may reveal. These personalities dissolve their attention into space and maintain a kind of emotional blandness, finding comfort in blunting the sharp edge of challenge.

'Spacing out' or strategic ignore-ance, is a numbing and dumbing strategy which temporarily removes the threat of change and choice. We attempt to cut off our sense fields because the space outside feels terrifying, as we become frozen in numbness or unresponsiveness and refuse to relate with anything.

Avalokiteshvara appears in the animal realm with a book because the animal personality lacks reflective thought which would liberate them from their instinctual or habitual patterns. The book symbolizes *prajna*, the heightened cognitive capacity to penetrate the animal realm personality's tendency towards inertia and spiritual laziness, and their effort to sabotage genuine change in themselves.

As animal realm personalities we have to be encouraged to develop passionate inquisitiveness to explore the space of our own being. This begins with bringing attention to our body in order to experience our sensations, feelings and instincts. Secondly, we need to stay with that particular experience long enough to recognize what we are actually feeling. The virtue of space is that when we do get in touch with our body and work through our particular core issues of dissociation and inertia, we can embrace our intrinsic worth.

Animal personalities have merged with their significant

others and their environments, and have not yet developed genuine individuality and autonomy. Consequently they would benefit by risking change and cutting through their inertia and ambivalence by leaning into the sharp edge of making decisions.

The *virtues* of the animal realm personality are innocence and simplicity. We transform inertia and self-forgetfulness into non-conceptual awareness, the wisdom of radical openness. This permits us to spontaneously initiate action without the interference of our ego. The power of indestructible space takes everything back to our original source, which is the silence and stillness of simple being, the wisdom of no point of view.

As if gazing at the open sky, we could simply be with our experience of this immediate moment in its totality. There's nothing to know conceptually, but rather such experience invites a sense of intelligent being and authentic presence. It is a radical openness to the unfolding of the present moment as well as to one's life in general. It is clear awareness of each moment without losing sight of the whole.

When we take our first step out the door in the morning rather than give in to our usual preoccupations, we could look out at the morning with fresh eyes and may notice a flower blooming through a crack in a broken fence. There is much human experience which is meant to be simply lived, where there's no need to figure anything out or achieve anything. We could learn to attune our being with the subtle energy and guidance of space. This is not a poetic sentiment.

If, as animal personalities, we dare to exercise inquiry or self-questioning, the dullness and inertia of performing daily routines can be broken up with humor and a spirit of play, permitting us to reconnect with the wisdom energy of space.

If we refuse to breathe flexibility into our routines and expand our range of behaviors, we may grow unreasonably hungry for stimuli. As if to compensate for all that we've missed, we may find ourselves in the *hungry ghost realm* at this point.

The Hungry Ghost Realm: Transforming the Poverty Stricken Personality

The hungry ghost realm is associated with the wisdom energy of earth which is symbolized by the autumnal harvest, the season of fruition and fulfillment. The earth element is connected with our natural capacity for growth and creativity, and with feelings of solidity, depth, fullness, richness and the substantiality of experience. Much like the earth itself which supports all manner of flora and fauna without bias, the wisdom aspect of the earth is *equanimity*, an unbiased approach to experience, where we respond freshly to each moment without preconceptions, expectations or judgments.

When we dissociate from these naturally existing qualities we inadvertently create an inner abyss which we then interpret as inner impoverishment and hollowness. As hungry ghost personalities, we experience a loss of connection with our roots, leaving us with a feeling of abandonment and a deprivation of natural resources. When we disconnect from the wisdom energy of earth, we try to imitate its natural qualities of richness, solidity and expansiveness, but feel dwarfed by the monumental quality of reality. Secretly, we feel weak and small in spite of our bravado.

According to Buddhist iconography, hungry ghosts are depicted as having stovepipe legs and arms, a spindly neck, a huge protruding belly and a tiny mouth the size of the eye of a needle. This being rummages through various landscapes gathering scraps of food, trying to feed itself, but can never get enough nourishment through its tiny mouth to fill its enormous belly.

The spectrum of suffering in the hungry ghost realm ranges from actual torment to chronic poverty mentality. At the extreme end of the spectrum, due to overwhelming craving, the body of the hungry ghost is deformed and he or she appears to be alien, never at home in the world. Feeling like a stranger in a strange land, the hungry ghost continuously feels empty and poverty stricken, and seeks 'nourishment' to fill his or her aching void, but can never get enough food, companionship, sex, entertainment or positive experience. No matter how much we consume we are left aching.

There is a humorous scene in one of Woody Allen's movies, where he's on a subway car that's populated by the downtrodden of New York's subway system. Everyone looks either asleep, depleted or drugged. As the train stops at the next station, Woody notices that across the tracks on another subway car, a party seems to be in full swing. Everyone is having joyful conversation, laughing and drinking champagne, while multicolored balloons float in the background. Looking completely deprived and forlorn, Woody gazes longingly at this tantalizing social scene.

This is a good metaphor for the hungry ghost personality, who is unable to find gratification with anyone or anything. No matter who we are with, no matter what we are doing, no matter what we get in life, we feel deprived, and yearn for relief from our hunger for companionship, wealth, opportunity, good health, or anything else we could imagine.

Our urgent hunger creates a flicker of hope when we think that our emptiness can be remedied. We may go to our favorite Mexican restaurant and get the super big chicken burrito with avocado and sour cream, hoping that this will bring satisfaction. As the food is brought to our table we begin salivating as we rub our hands together in gleeful anticipation.

We devour our burrito, barely savoring its flavors or delighting in its different textures. Having savagely consumed our meal, we now feel bloated and soon our stomach begins to hurt. Satisfaction was momentary and soon turns to nausea and abdominal distress. We might become acutely aware that we are sitting alone, while the restaurant is populated by couples and families, all of whom seem to be enjoying each other's company. This perception sends a dagger through our heart as we feel the continued echo of abandonment and desolation. At that point we may force ourselves to vomit to relieve our distress.

The *demons* in meditation and life for the hungry ghost personality are unsatisfied hunger for 'nourishment' and chronic feelings of emptiness. As hungry ghost personalities, we struggle to compensate for our disconnection from the earth qualities of solidity and richness. We try by make ourselves feel more substantial by accentuating our richness through indiscriminate consumption and overindulgence, but the nagging feeling of hollowness drives us to pursue further sources of gratification.

The *pathological extreme* for this realm could be associated with either *bipolar* or *borderline* personality disorders, as well as addictions of all types and varieties. The basic feature of the borderline personality is a pattern of unstable relationships, which often alternate between extremes of idealization and devaluation. We initially put new friends and loved ones on the top of our mountain and then abruptly demote them to the dungeons of hell because of their perceived flaws.

Borderline individuals suffer from identity disturbance due to an unstable sense of self, and could feel like strangers in a strange land like the hungry ghost. They make frantic efforts to avoid real or imagined abandonment and the feeling of desolation that would follow from such rejection. These desperate efforts lead to emotionally intense relationships, which often end dramatically and abruptly, giving them exactly what they are trying to avoid.

The other pathological extreme is bipolar disorder, those individuals whose thought and behavior alternates between manic and depressive cycles. Alternating between euphoria and irritability and depression, bipolar disordered individuals might swing from indiscriminate enthusiasm for relationships and novel experiences, followed by feelings of depletion, boredom and depression, as if the air were suddenly let out of their celebratory balloon.

The hungry ghost personality suffers repeated cycles of

momentary hope, a glimmer of satisfaction, followed by a dismal return to aching emptiness. Avalokiteshvara appears in this realm carrying a receptacle of sacred food and drink to liberate hungry ghosts from their torment. He teaches them to transmute their neurotic craving into a desire for the dharma, the wisdom teachings of the Buddha.

With the exception of the pathological extremes of borderline or bipolar personality disorders, (who require therapy and possibly medication), as hungry ghosts, our hunger for stimulation and gratification can be transformed into sobriety and gratitude. Through the practice of loving kindness, as we reconnect with our own depths we find delight in our own richness and fullness. Unlovability, shame and neediness are transformed into appreciation of our basic worthiness and lovability. It is only from a sense of self-appreciation that we stop hungering for something outside of us to fill us up.

Earth is connected with our body, our sensations, feelings, and instincts, which are bridges between our interior world and the external world. Earth represents our capacity to *feel into* the richness and substantiality of our experience without trying to make personal territory out of it. We allow all manner of experience to coexist, the good, the bad, the ugly and the beautiful without grasping or rejecting such experiences. We may develop a balanced state of mind and experience the inner support of earth.

When we actually touch our own inner earth we feel that there is something unshakable that can't be manipulated. We discover that this unconditioned substantial quality is *who* we genuinely are. This allows us to embody the virtue of earth, equanimity, an unbiased view of ourselves and others.

As hungry ghosts we must become mindful that we tend to intensify feelings of loss through our imagination. The contradiction is that our chronic feelings of loss and abandonment permit us to feel more alive and so we are irresistibly drawn to drama. In order to transform our suffering we need to become aware of how our feelings of loss and emptiness are perpetuated by ignoring whatever or whoever is within our reach. Instead, we tend to focus on the negative aspects of situations. Finally, we must overcome the fear that we will lose ourselves if we surrender our suffering.

If we persist in our folly as hungry ghost personalities, we become completely exhausted and demoralized from reaching for external sources of consolation, only to experience renewed feelings of hollowness. If we are unable or unwilling to dissolve our fixation on impoverishment we may grow increasingly angry and resentful that the world is unfair and punitive. This mentality could degenerate into the hell realm, the most horrific of all the realms.

The Hell Realm: The Tormented Personality

The hell realm personality is associated with the wisdom energy of water which refers to the reflective quality of water's surface. It is perception that is clear, brilliant, and transparent, as well as purifying, in that its clarity cleanses us of cognitive distortions. Water's fluidity allows it to make contact with everything in its current without holding onto anything. Water's reflectiveness honors every nuance and detail of its surrounding environment 'seeing' it as a seamless whole.

As hell realm personalities, we suffer the misperception that the penetrating clarity and sharpness of raw experience will pierce our protective armor and we will find ourselves embarrassingly visible. When we dissociate from the awakened quality of the water element within us, we immediately lose our capacity for panoramic reflection. To compensate for this disconnection from our inner water element, we use conceptual thinking as a defense to keep life distant from us. The reflective clarity of water now becomes frozen, as we lose our capacity to flow with the fluidity of events.

The hell realm, as with all the six realms, has a spectrum of possible expressions. In its more extreme or chronic form, this overly conceptual frame of mind holds its perspective rigidly and uses anger to defend itself from life situations that feel threatening. By freezing the water element's fluidity, we fragment both ourselves and the world. Frozen water is sharp and jagged, and is used by the hell realm personality to 'cut through' others' perspectives with anger, freezing all communication.

As hell realm personalities, we live with a desperation to manipulate reality to make it fit our distorted version of things. We are obsessively attached to doing things a certain way or for events and situations to unfold in a specific manner. If we perceive an error or mistake, we feel that such 'wrongdoing' must be fixed or punished as our world has become highly polarized between right and wrong, good and evil.

From such confusion and bewilderment, we believe that we are isolated within our own consciousness, bounded by the skin-encapsulated body. As a defense against deep feeling, we create a conceptual system of abstract thought to map out reality, filtering out inconvenient facts.

'Hell' is feeling cut off from the wellspring of life, feeling disconnected from our body, our feelings, intuitions and our depths. We sharply divide the world into warring camps, losing contact with the innate wisdom of life's fluidity. As hell realm personalities, we do not want anyone to see us beyond our imaginary persona and so we are fearful of too much visibility, of being penetrated by the truth. We respond with cold aggression which invites retaliation or rejection, provoking further aggression or retreat from the world.

The basic theme of the hell realm is the torment that results from feeling trapped in no-exit situations. The maddening aspect of this realm is that as ferociously as we try to lash out at our identified enemies or at adversarial situations, our own anger seems to bounce back at us, thickening the walls of our self-imposed prison. This in turn, causes us to become even more infuriated and escalates our rage.

Although few of us suffer from this torturous mentality, we could use this description to understand the futility of anger and aggression. Imagine that someone close to you has unexpectedly betrayed you and offers no explanation or apology. During this same period of time, someone at work who is junior to you, has been outshining you in her work performance, and you've just learned that your boss is giving your position to her. To complicate matters, the inheritance that you were expecting to receive from your grandmother has run into a snag. Much to your dismay, you learn that she has disowned you, because your relatives have been speaking poorly about you to her hoping to get a larger share of the inheritance.

Sometimes our life becomes surrealistic in that a number of disappointments or betrayals congeal to completely demoralize and infuriate us. There are no easy solutions to any of the above situations and we could feel furiously angry that somehow the world has conspired against us. If we have been victimized or physically or emotionally abused, or if we've been repeatedly betrayed, rejected or abandoned especially early in life, we could develop the distortions of the hell realm personality.

Some individuals become severely depressed or traumatized and are rendered immobile and defenseless, while others become outraged, and lash out at their imagined assailants. In our angry or rageful state of mind, we create sparks in our encounters with others, provoking negative reactions from them, which would further inflame us. This is a taste of hell.

The *demons* in meditation and life for the hell realm personality are suspicion, paranoia, intensely negative judgments, anger and aggression. We are fearful of being invaded, undermined or overwhelmed by others. Consequently, we monitor the environment for threats to our vulnerable sense of self, as we attempt to justify and rationalize all experience within our distorted conceptual system.

The *pathological extreme* associated with the hell realm personality is paranoid schizophrenia, which is characterized by delusions and/or hallucinations related to suspicions of persecution. This is often a basis for the hell realm individual's explosions of anger and violence. There is a pervasive fear of being engulfed by oceanic feelings or invaded by the outside world. When threats are detected, water in its distorted form, reacts with anger, attempting to push the world away. Like boiling water, the hell realm personality can be hot with anger or like ice, sharp and cutting.

Avalokiteshvara, motivated by great compassion, descends to the deepest hell. He holds the mirror of knowledge with which he transforms the cognitive distortions of hell beings into reflective clarity and precision, so that they may recognize how they are projecting their delusional belief system onto the world. Hell realm personalities learn to cut through their conceptualized version of situations so that the energy of anger is not manipulated to protect their system of thought. The energy of anger has the potential to sharpen their immediate presence, as they release their delusional narrative. This transforms the energy of anger into undistorted clarity.

With loving support and gentle non-threatening communication, such personalities may begin doubting their paranoid thoughts. They may eventually learn to discriminate delusional thoughts from those that are an accurate reflection of the world as it is. Feedback from trusted others are essential for a process of healing to occur.

It would be optimal if the hell realm personality could trust in a loving community, whose members embody gentleness, kindness and compassion. Through such 're-parenting', hell realm personalities may learn to be kinder and gentler with themselves, eventually having glimpses of their own basic goodness. Their delusions and hallucinations could be normalized in group therapy with others who suffer from similar symptoms. Eventually positive steps could be made towards holding a job, establishing meaningful relationships or simply finding gratification in ordinary pleasurable activities.

As hell realm personalities at the higher end of the spectrum, we suffer more from a pattern of reactive anger and a rigid manner of thinking. We must recognize how our own inflexibility and defensiveness creates a prison for ourselves, causing us to feel alienated from others. Instead of holding on for dear life to our point of view, we might practice 'melting' rather than freezing. As we learn to relax our defenses, there is the momentary clear sighting of transparent water.

We must work with our body and our sensations and feelings. Relaxation melts the rigidity of ice and allows us to become fluid. The positive aspect of the water element is that when it flows, it breaks up any fixed perspective that we may be holding.

Like water's mirror-like reflection, we allow ourselves to accurately *reflect* the truth of situations, rather than defending against them. Like the fluidity of water, we make deeper contact with our body's natural rhythms, and we become capable of moving playfully with the currents of situations. We need to accept the imperfection of the world as well as our own imperfection. This would involve accepting a whole spectrum of feelings to be experienced without feeling that we are being contaminated.

As hell realm personalities, we may grow wise by gradually loosening our defenses and paranoia in order to establish gratifying friendships, and perhaps could transition out of this horrific realm into a less tormented place. However, if we continue to solidify our delusions, feeling continually threatened by invasion and infiltration by an alien world of others, then we are left with no choice but to go completely mad.

The Human Realm: The Pleasure-Oriented Personality

The human realm is associated with the wisdom energy of fire. Fire's radiance illuminates our true condition by distinguishing one thing from another, clarifying samsara from nirvana, and neurosis from sanity. This aspect of the awakened mind reveals the meaning of our experiences, bringing understanding and insight. The heat of the fire element magnetizes others towards us and promotes intimacy in relationship and empathy in our communication, transforming passion into compassion.

When we forget our true nature, we disconnect from the awakened quality of the fire element within us and give birth to the *human realm* personality. We now use passion and desire to *imitate* the wisdom qualities of the fire element. The cognitive distortion is our nagging feeling of emptiness and boredom. In reaction to this we use our fire energy as a compensation to draw others into our space to remedy these feelings. The fire element is associated with obsession, seduction and indiscriminate consumption of people, things or experiences, all of which promise to fill our loneliness and boredom.

When the Buddha proclaimed the four noble truths, he addressed desire as the cause of all suffering. He was referring to the desire that is ignorant of our original identity. We have the innate power of discernment and choice, but our restless imagination seduces us to seek ever more subtle and refined pleasures.

The intelligence, refined sensitivity and freedom of choice of the human realm actually drive it into neurosis. Unlike the other realms, the human realm personality is aware of impending death and this creates anxiety and unrest. All the other realms except for human mentality are solid blocks of preoccupation and struggle, where beings feel trapped in an atmosphere of conflict and do not have the luxury of choice.

The human realm personality has such sensitivity that we perceive the alternation between pleasure and pain, hope and fear, as well as the space between the perceiver and the perceived. These alternations or gaps create self-doubt, and make us less certain, but our imagination more fluid. Due to our intolerance of boredom, we can become so distracted with one inconsequential project after another, that we spill our energy, and exhaust ourselves.

Imagine driving your luxury car down a freeway on a beautiful sunny day. You decide to open the sunroof to enhance the pleasure of driving on the open road. You do so, but notice that the music from your car CD player is not clear and crisp, and so you decide to close the sunroof to eliminate the noise from the highway. You then discover that it is getting rather warm in your vehicle, so you turn on the air conditioner. You adjust the air conditioning several times, but can't get the internal temperature just quite right, and soon you feel the threat of a headache.

You now decide that if you move into the right lane and go slower, you'll be able to open up a window and still be able to hear your music, as well as enjoy a view of the rolling green pastures. You have succeeded in maximizing your pleasure, but wonder if you will arrive late to your destination, now that you're traveling at a reduced speed. For the remainder of your journey, you alternate between enjoying the ride and silently struggling with whether to change lanes or not, or re-open the sunroof or turn on the air conditioner.

The human realm personality, always pushing to make the situation a little bit more stimulating, delightful, or more comfortable, continually adjusts either itself or the environment to get maximum delight. The continual search for pleasure and comfort creates its own problem, for it is followed by the shadow of eventual dissatisfaction and unrest.

The *demons* that plague the human realm mentality, in both meditation and in life, are fear of mortality, obsessive desire, and the tendency to catastrophize. Because we can anticipate a future, we can imagine everything that could go wrong, and this creates anxiety. Our freedom of choice opens up the possibilities for pleasure and pain, success and failure, and this provokes the search for greatest pleasure and ultimate freedom, heaven, paradise, enlightenment! This is the problem and the promise.

The *pathological extreme* in the human realm are anxiety and stress disorders, where we worry excessively about the stuff of ordinary life, such as our work performance, our health, our safety and security, or catastrophic things happening to our children or our intimates. Alternately, we might experience the stress of launching our ambition to create a more abundant life or successful career.

Yet, feelings of emptiness, incompleteness and loneliness might plague us as we seek happiness and success, while trying to avoid pain and failure. We don't realize that we have co-opted the energy of fire and are expressing it as ordinary desire, as we try to 'consume' happiness or success as if they were external to us. Acting on such a belief reinforces our impoverishment.

In the iconographical painting of the Wheel of Life, Avalokiteshvara appears in the human realm as the Buddha with a staff and begging bowl to demonstrate the way of desire-lessness, which is the wisdom of acceptance and 'letting be'. This is precisely the antidote for our neurotic desire. We allow our lives to unfold, cultivating trust and appreciation that things are evolving as they should. Such acceptance minimizes the impulse to manipulate our experience in an effort to enhance our pleasure or defend ourselves from life's unavoidable twists and turns.

The *virtue* of the human realm is that, unlike the other realms, we are aware that we're going to die. Although we try to deny this realization as best we can, we're left with the haunting reminder of our mortality, which draws our human life into sharp perspective. The increased intelligence and sensitivity of human mentality permits a more accurate assessment of our true condition. We might find ourselves contemplating the big questions: "What is the purpose, if any, of my human life?"

"What is of enduring value in an impermanent universe?" "How should I best use my energy to promote the greatest good?"

Only in the human realm do we give birth to the idea of meditation. Through meditation practice we might have the insight that almost all of our desires are motivated by a sense of deficiency, the feeling that whatever I have or whoever I am, it's just not enough. We commonly assume that this present moment is not enough, and that we need something to fill ourselves, to make us feel more satisfied, complete, and whole.

Meditation reveals that such deficiency-based desire repeatedly ignores *this* living moment, and that this ignore-ance is the source of human unhappiness. Desirelessness in this case, means that we don't allow ourselves to be seduced by the thought that there is a better moment in the future.

The alchemical process of transformation is where we learn to *hold* the energy of desire and not dramatize it by immediately fulfilling it. We practice holding the fire of our own passion in order to sense its meaning and direction. This is in direct contrast to the tendency to either repress or dramatize our desires.

The brilliant energy of fire illuminates the merits of both ourselves and others beyond our demand that we or they be different. Instead, we radiate appreciation to clarify the uniqueness of both ourselves and others. The intense radiation of the light of the fire element reveals that ultimately, all desire seeks to be united with our source in love, to return home, where we no longer experience the pain of separation.

When we hold the energy of desire, we can sense our avoidance of ourselves and our denial of the world as it is. We counter the impulse to spill our life force through desire by expressing appreciation and clarity, discerning samsaric from nirvanic possibilities.

Of the six realms, only as inhabitants of the human realm, do we have the chance to wake up spiritually and actually become enlightened. Because we momentarily notice the space between ourselves and our projections, we have a chance to see the world as *it is*, not as we would like it to be. This permits us to work with the force of karmic cause and effect as we refrain from manipulating situations to be other than what they are.

One of the mixed blessings of the human realm is the Promethean desire to steal 'fire from the gods'. Enough is never enough, as the human intelligence reaches for the superlative. We can embark on a spiritual path to reconnect with our essential nature or we can manufacture the idea of heaven, permanent paradise, the ultimate salvation for our stress and worry, where we are buffered from the awareness of our necessary mortality. If we're seduced by this alternative, we're back on the wheel of samsara for yet another round of ceaseless struggle.

Epilogue: Heaven Earth and Humanity

In ancient Asian culture, the principle of heaven symbolized the sacred or exalted aspect of mind and its visionary possibilities, whereas the principle of earth, representing the qualities of receptivity and practicality, embodied those immaterial possibilities in the tangible forms of the natural world. The patriarchal principle of 'man' symbolized the challenge to humanity, to both men and women, to integrate the mandate of heaven within the cultural forms of human society.

If a society lived in harmony with the sacred vision of heaven and in sympathetic connection with nature, it was believed that it would flourish. If a society ignored its sacred connection with heaven and earth, it would amount to an act of violence against the natural order and lead to social chaos and natural disaster.

We are presently facing the threat of what many climatologists are calling the 'sixth great extinction', as there have been five previous massive waves of extinction according to the geological record. We are witnessing unparalleled environmental degradation, ever increasing global warming, species extinction, resource depletion, increasing militarization and the proliferation of nuclear weapons, and a growing disparity between the rich industrialized northern nations and the poorer developing nations of the south.

These ecological and social problems are different aspects of one crisis, which is based on our distorted image and experience of ourselves as skin-encapsulated egos, who are separate and different from the natural world. We are suffering from a *crisis of perception* which has lead to a conspicuous lack of humanistic values that would ensure our survival.

Feeling separation and disconnection from our world, we suffer emptiness or psychological impoverishment that prompts us to endlessly consume 'goods' (money, food, and sex) to fill our aching void. We believe that we must struggle to survive in a competitive Darwinian socio-economic jungle, and feeling threatened by others, we resort to aggression to protect our imagined boundaries and to expand our territory. We have become so disconnected from others that reports of environmental destruction and human suffering leave us emotionally unaffected or numb.

The myth of perpetual economic progress supports the belief that to survive well, there must be endless production and consumption. The conspicuous flaw in this paradigm is that the economy has become the preeminent institution of modern society, as we have monetized and quantified every aspect of human existence. Economic logic and values, not the mandate of heaven, have become the primary guides to our collective decision making. We treat the earth and other human beings not as sacred embodiments of life, but as *resources* to be used in the service of the economy.

There is a pervasive denial of karmic cause and effect, as First World nations ignore the implicit relation between their actions, in the name of progress, and the resulting consequences. There seems to be no recognition of the need to submit to anything beyond our own mind-made ideologies.

It is interesting to speculate how Buddha would weigh in on these macro problems threatening our very survival. When presented with such global concerns, Buddha might ask us the deceptively simple question, "What is a flower?" We would probably begin by describing the conventional notion of a flower as a plant which is comprised of its colorful petals, leaves and stem. The Buddha might look at us inquiringly as if asking, "Is that all?"

We might then consider the soil from which a flower grows without which there would be no flower. In our consideration of the soil, we must include in our description of a flower, the millions of decomposed flora and fauna whose bodies have become nutrients for all flowers. Our response would probably be met by Buddha's continued inquiring gaze.

Perhaps with some prompting we might recognize that we must include the sun and its radiation of light and warmth that sustains all life on earth. Part of our description would include the sun's power to evaporate water from our planet's lakes, streams, and oceans to form clouds which pour down life-generating rain to fertilize the earth. It may slowly dawn upon us that to define a flower or any living entity we must include the whole universe. To think otherwise, is to artificially exile ourselves from sympathetic relationship with the vast networks of the natural world.

Buddha taught that the primary source of suffering, confusion and destructive behavior in the world was due to our identification with the separate ego-self. He recommended mindfulness practice to help us see through this illusion, permitting an intuition of our implicit connection with the surrounding world. This notion of interconnectedness is made explicit in the Buddha's doctrine of *codependent origination* which clarifies that all phenomena, plant and animal, animate and inanimate, are mutually interdependent and mutually interpenetrating, each drawing sustenance from the whole.

Of significance, this Buddhist teaching emphasizes awareness as an intrinsic part of the whole system, without which there is no system, no entities, nothing to perceive at all. In other words, the visible network of animals, plants, mountains and streams, is brought forth by our intrinsic awareness, making us co-creators of the "10, 000 things".

The Buddhist teaching of egolessness may be parallel to the wider ecological sense of self that includes the entire natural world *and* the planetary intelligence that regulates it. The Buddhist contribution to our survival as a species lies in its radical shift away from our distorted image of ourselves as disconnected from the natural world, to an appreciation of our *identity* with it. Buddhism provides the means by which we can have an actual experience of this through the practice of mindfulness and awareness.

We might look at the ecological implications of the *three jewels*, the Buddha, the dharma, and the sangha. In the most liberal sense of the word, we could think of Buddha, not only as the historical Indian prince who attained enlightenment, but as Buddha essence, the formless intelligence behind the natural world's self-regulating, self-balancing, self-correcting systems.

This vision of Buddha essence finds resonance in the ecological perspective which views the earth as a self-organizing, self-regulating, self-balancing living system. This system is sustained through sympathetic interaction among and between all of its parts, none of which is separate from the planetary intelligence that animates all living systems. It follows that *we* are also self-organizing and self-balancing systems who are sustained through sympathetic interaction with all of the living earth.

This view challenges our feelings of alienation and inner poverty, from which the motive of exploitation arises. It can lead to an understanding that all true growth is based on experiencing an ever-widening sense of self that transcends our individual body-mind and includes the surrounding natural world, and eventually the planet itself.

If we consider the dharma, the second of the three jewels, in the widest possible sense, it is the 'teaching' revealed in the patterns of nature itself. The phenomenal world contains innumerable metaphors pregnant with suggestions for how we can be in right relationship with each other and with life. The migration pattern of birds, the pollination of flowers by bees, the cyclical rhythm of the seasons and the tides, and the orderly progression of the planets around us, all suggest an image of mind as an open self-organizing, self-balancing intelligence.

This is a potent suggestion that we, as individuals, are in

continual two way communication with our world. We are penetrated by the currents of matter, energy and information from the surrounding environment, and there is no definitive line separating a solid, continuous self from the network, and yet personal identity is not extinguished either.

Sangha, the third of the three jewels, in the widest possible sense, is the community of all living beings and not only humans. Sangha is comprised of animals, plants, insects, bees, earth, ocean and sky, and all the diverse human communities across the planet. These populations work to produce our pants and shirts, computers and cars, as well as the food on our dinner table. We are fully interdependent with these global communities for the commodities which we use every day.

There's also the cultural exchange and transmission of ideas, language, philosophy and religion, art and music, and our social and cultural networks that bring us new ideas, frames of perception, values and models of behavior.

From the perspective of egoless intelligence, we can more easily grasp our interconnection with the entire world. The protection of Mother Nature would be felt as protection of ourselves. We might realize in a deep way, that we are all stewards of the earth and its inhabitants. We're not truly free until we transform the social and political institutions that are responsible for raping our Mother, marginalizing the economically impoverished, and criminalizing the needs of the disenfranchised due to race, gender or class.

One of the most distorted aspects of the prevailing contemporary paradigm is the failure to recognize the disparity between our outer material and technological progress and our inner evolution. It is a failure to recognize that inner growth is essential to our human evolutionary process and our survival as a species.

Let us conclude by returning to where this book began, with simple mindfulness of breath as a form of guidance from heaven and earth. If we consider this simple process of breathing, we might discover profound wisdom in this natural activity. We learn that in order to *get* a fresh breath of air, we must *give up* a breath, as exhalation precedes inhalation. To sacrifice is to "make sacred" and is the lawful activity of life itself. From this we begin to intuitively understand that we cannot continue limitless expansion by depleting resources, without putting back something in equal measure to nourish the cycle of life.

By bringing our mindful attention to the process of breathing, we can't help but notice that everything changes, and that nothing stays the same. Our belief that 'I' is an unchanging identical self might become highly suspect as mindfulness invites deeper scrutiny, taking us to the boundary where self meets no-self.

Thirdly, we discover that change itself has a rhythm or pattern like the oceanic tides and the progression of the seasons, and is not random or chaotic. We might develop trust that beyond our strategic effort to control ourselves, significant others, and the natural world, there is a larger rhythm that promotes balance and harmony through the sustained tension of order and chaos.

Lastly, we may recognize that we are *being breathed* and this might lead to a deep intuition that our lives are animated by an intelligent energy that transcends our limited ego-self, but is the very essence of *who* we are. This intelligence provides continual guidance for how to live in harmony with heaven and earth, but it must be respected. To live with such respect is to live in a sacred world.

References

1 Simone Weil, *Formative Writings* (Abigton, UK: Routledge Revivals, 1964), Edited and translated by DT MacFarland and W. Van Ness. p. 200

2 Elaine Pagels, *The Gnostic Gospels* (New York: Vintage Books, 1981) p.152

(as quoted from the Nag Hammadi Library (New York, 1977) p. 21

CHANGE
MAKERS
BOOKS

Changemakers publishes books for individuals committed to transforming their lives and transforming the world. Our readers seek to become positive, powerful agents of change. Changemakers books inform, inspire, and provide practical wisdom and skills to empower us to create the next chapter of humanity's future.

Please visit our website at www.changemakers-books.com